GENDERED WORK IN ASIAN CITIES

Gendered Work in Asian Cities
The New Economy and Changing Labour Markets

ANN BROOKS

ASHGATE

Published by

Ashgate Publishing Limited
Gower House
Croft Road
Aldershot
Hampshire GU11 3HR
England

Ashgate Publishing Company
Suite 420
101 Cherry Street
Burlington, VT 05401-4405
USA

Ashgate website: http://www.ashgate.com

British Library Cataloguing in Publication Data
Brooks, Ann, 1952-
  Gendered work in Asian cities : the new economy and
  changing labour markets
  1.Women - Employment - Asia 2.Professional employees - Asia
  3.Sex role in the work environment - Asia 4.Women - Social
  conditions - Asia
  I.Title
  331.4'095

Library of Congress Cataloging-in-Publication Data
Brooks, Ann, 1952-
  Gendered work in Asian cities : the new economy and changing labour markets / by Ann Brooks.
      p. cm.
  Includes bibliographical references and index.
  ISBN 978-0-7546-4700-3
 1. Discrimination in employment--China--Hong Kong. 2. Discrimination in employment--Singapore. 3. Discrimination in employment--Asia. 4. Women in the professions--China--Hong Kong. 5. Women in the professions--Singapore. 6. Women in the professions--Asia. 7. Sex discrimination against women--China--Hong Kong. 8. Sex discrimination against women--Singapore. 9. Sex discrimination against women--Asia. 10. Globalization. I. Title.

  HD6060.5.C62H662 2005
  331.4'133095--dc22

                                                                    2005026481

ISBN 978-0-7546-4700-3

Reprinted 2007

Printed and bound in Great Britain by MPG Books Ltd. Bodmin, Cornwall.

Contents

Foreword

Asia has seen remarkable change in the last two decades, moving to the centre of the globalizing world economy. One of the most notable aspects of these changes has been the rise of new middle classes across the region. Yet the gender dimensions of these transformations continue to be overlooked in too many of the key texts exploring these changes. Ann Brooks' book on professional women in Hong Kong and Singapore therefore is a very welcome addition to the literature on women and gender in Asia. Until now there has been no book-length study of the working lives of upper middle-class professional women in Asia, apart from Jean Renshaw's study of women managers in Japan (1999).

Ann Brooks' book explores in some detail the impact of the new economy on the relationship between gender and specific professional labour markets in the two global cities of Hong Kong and Singapore. These two cities, she tells us, have the highest numbers of professional women in Asia. A key strength of the book is the way Ann Brooks explores the gender dimensions of organizational and social change in Asia against a wider background discussion of globalization, gender and social change in the region. She poses some key issues to frame her discussion, including the implications of globalization and the growth of the 'new economy' for transnational labour markets: she sees transnationalism as having important gendered dimensions. Quoting Saskia Sassen, she points us to the ways in which the space constituted by the global grid of cities, a space with new economic and political potentialities, is perhaps one of the most strategic spaces for the formation of transnational identities and communities. Both the Hong Kong and the Singapore governments have adopted an open-door policy to attract both global foreign talent and female domestic labour: the latter is a highly significant player within this changing order, as Brooks emphasizes.

This choice of locations for Brooks' empirical study highlights some significant developments vital in understanding the gendered character of globalization: the growing differentiation within the division of labour between, and within gender frameworks; the growing 'feminization' of job supply and of business opportunities; the increased access to wages and salaries for women at both the upper and lower ends of the market; changing gender hierarchies; increased mobility at the high and low ends of the job market; and the increased prominence of women both as visible 'power-brokers' and as significant consumers within the global economy.

She raises some interesting and important questions about the impact of organizational and societal change on the lives of professional women in these two cities. She is particularly interested in asking whether globalization and the growth of the global knowledge economy have opened up more opportunities for professional women in organizational life. What are the positives and negatives for women of corporate restructuring, the 'new managerialism', and increased 'flexibility' in organizational structures? What issues exist around leadership and management for professional women in organizations? And what organizational styles are still the preferred or dominant ones in organizations? Are they still characterized by the 'cultures of masculinity' described by other authors? To what extent are women leaders and managers acceptable within organizational cultures, and as acceptable to male and female employees? She is concerned to identify both the organizational factors and the wider global factors that can be identified as advancing the position of women in leadership and management and in hindering such advancement, and takes us through some cases of her informants involvement in leadership in education and in politics. Her findings, in fact, show that where they do achieve leadership positions, women are confident, capable leaders. She concludes that the obstacles to women's advancement in both organizational life and in academia in both cities parallel those reported in the West, although the close links between corporate families and business have allowed women in Hong Kong and Singapore to capitalize on these to some extent and reach higher levels of corporate life.

She also wants to know to what extent equal opportunities and anti-discrimination are addressed in legislative frameworks in Hong Kong and Singapore and debated within social policy debates there. To look at their impact on social policy debates, and patterns of social change in both cities, she takes us through a discussion of demographic patterns, including fertility rates, marriage patterns, numbers of children, and the proportions of singles and married at different ages as well as the numbers of women in workforce. She also details the involvement of some of her informants in such legislative change, including the Bill of Rights and equal opportunity legislation in Hong Kong: such developments may account for a greater willingness by her informants there to apply a gender analysis than she found in Singapore.

A particular strength of the book is the way it gives us a direct insight into professional women's everyday lives in both cities through the interviews with her sample. As Brooks describes them, the personal and social issues confronting professional women in senior positions are formidable. She explores the concerns raised for professional women around being single, marriage and family obligations, spousal attitudes to career, parenting /care giving and household, attitudes to spouse/ partner's career, and support structures in the home to assist women in their career. The book illustrates well the dynamics of the evolving relationships between 'family' expectations and actually lived experiences of many of these professional women. It also illustrates some of the heated cultural politics surrounding women, work and family in both cities, not least the continuing heritage of Confucianism. In both places, the media have been energetic in discussing single women and low birth rates. Although the cultural assumptions are that 'career' women are mostly single, Brooks in fact found that this stereotype is the exception rather than the rule. Many such women were married and inevitably involved in often precarious work/life balancing acts. While work is an increasing source of identity for many of her informants, in Hong Kong, for example, women faced a backlash from the media: in the face of the economic downturn in 2001 fears were promoted that husbands would turn to other women if successful women failed to cope with their roles as wives and mothers. The book is especially useful in exploring women's experiences in their own words, and providing us with developed pictures of the complex working lives of a sample of women. It evokes some poignant personal issues and decisions faced by some of Brooks' informants. We hear first hand about husbands who are reported to be supportive to varying degrees, of the complex domestic negotiations involved in making work and home balance to any degree, and of competition between husbands and wives. The women still wanted husbands to be involved in domesticity, even though 'maids' did much of the actual work, but not too involved, in some cases.

This highlights the key issue of migrant domestic labour. Brooks is very interested in the role of such labour in serving the needs of advanced economies. As she points out, global cities are where we find the most highly paid and the lowest paid workers. Such workers have few civil rights in either Singapore or Hong Kong. She sees opportunities for professional women greatly facilitated by the employment of such workers in both cities. Such employment clearly offsets the need for organisations to provide childcare facilities and become 'family-friendly firms', and forestalls domestic negotiations around housework and childcare.

As Brooks emphasizes, her interviewees are a significant group, women explicitly chosen because they had views and had something to say about the world as they saw it: many are critical commentators who have written about issues concerned with social and cultural change in the region or have been involved in formulating change in the corporate academic and political world and cultural worlds; they are women who have reflected on their own position and been professionally involved in producing social change. While the book concludes that there have been some improvements in gender equality in Asia, much remains to be done. Her informants are energetically involved both in chronicling the changing order in the region and in reshaping the debates around such change. This book will be of great interest to those concerned with both these changes and the wider globalizing order.

Maila Stivens
Director of Gender Studies
University of Melbourne

References

Jean R. Renshaw, *Kimono in the Boardroom: The Invisible Evolution of Japanese Women Managers* (New York: Oxford University Press, 1999).

Acknowledgements

I would like to acknowledge the support and enthusiasm of a number of people in this project. Firstly I would like to thank Massey University for the research funding which supported the empirical research in Asia. I would also like to acknowledge Professor Robyn Munford (Massey University) for her support of my research. In addition Professor Allan Luke (NIE/NTU, Singapore and the University of Queensland), Professor Maila Stivens (University of Melbourne) and Associate Professor Ryan Bishop (National University of Singapore) have been enthusiastic and untiring supporters of my work.

At Ashgate Publishers, I would particularly like to thank the editors Mary Savigar and Caroline Wintersgill for their keen support of the book and the entire editorial and production team for making the process effortless.

Finally the book would not have been possible without the contributions of the outstanding women from academic and corporate life in Singapore and Hong Kong who made the process of research a thoroughly rewarding, inspiring and collegial experience. I do hope this work does them justice. Last but not least my deepest thanks to Josette Balsa in Hong Kong who opened so many doors.

Dr Ann Brooks
Singapore 2005

Notes on the Author

Dr Ann Brooks has published extensively in the areas of globalization, gender and organizational change, citizenship and social justice, academic women and equity, contemporary feminist theory, cultural theory and sociology, postcolonialism and feminism. She is author of *Academic Women* (Open University Press, 1997); *Postfeminisms: Feminism, Cultural Theory and Cultural Forms* (Routledge, 1997); and with Alison Mackinnon *Gender and the Restructured University: Changing Management and Culture in Higher Education* (Open University Press, 2001). Dr Brooks spent the period between 1993-2002 as a Senior Lecturer in Sociology at Massey University, New Zealand. She relocated to Singapore in 2002 and is currently Head of Psychology and Sociology Programmes at SIM University in Singapore. This, her latest book, is based on research undertaken in Singapore and Hong Kong. Her most recent research and publication is located at the intersecting nexus of contemporary theorizing within gender and feminism particularly in exploring the relationship between intimacy and reflexivity in the construction of the gendered self. Her particular interest is in the construction of the self within late modernity in relation to professional and personal domains and involves a critique of theorists such as Beck and Giddens. She is also writing a co-edited textbook entitled *Sociology: Asian Perspectives*.

Introduction: Globalization
and the New Dynamics of Inequality

This book explores the impact of globalization, and the growth of the new economy on specific professional labour markets in Asia. More specifically the book seeks to examine the impact of these processes on professional women in the context of organizational and social change in Asia. Two global cities in Asia, Hong Kong and Singapore, form the focus of the empirical research on professional women but the debate as a whole is more broadly contextualized within an analysis of globalization, gender and social change in the region. The book raises a number of issues which are significant for professional women who are located within increasingly differentiated labour markets producing a 'new dynamics of inequality' and new urban economies. Professional women are one of a number of groups located at the intersecting nexus of globalization, gender and social change. The questions raised by this book include: What are the implications for gendered labour markets of globalization and the growth of the 'new economy'? Does globalization and the growth of the global knowledge economy present new opportunities for professional women? What implications does the growth of the 'new economy' have on transnational labour markets? What is the impact of globalization for women in the region more generally? The focus of the empirical research on professional women is centered on the global cities of Hong Kong and Singapore. Both Hong Kong and Singapore, while very different, see themselves as highly significant centers for the region in a number of ways. Both have positioned themselves as 'market leaders' in terms of the 'new economies', and as 'global knowledge hubs' for the growth of the global knowledge economy. Both centers are experiencing rapid social change, set against a backdrop of economic and political change. Professional women from the academic and corporate sectors were interviewed in Hong Kong and Singapore as a benchmark for assessing change, not only in terms of their own lives and organizational contexts, but also for assessing the intersection of globalization, gender and social change in the region. This book examines some of the theoretical underpinnings of the debates around globalization, gender and social change, combined with the findings of empirical research on professional women in Hong Kong and Singapore.

Globalization and the New Dynamics of Inequality

In her powerful analysis of the relationship between globalization, gender and social change, Sassen (1998) examines the relationship between the globalization of labour flows, frequently captured in the conceptualization of the transmigration of labour, and the new dynamics of inequality. Sassen shows that the impact of globalization on labour migration is part of the same process as the development of global finance and global capital. Her analysis of these processes draws attention to the new dynamics of inequality, framed by the growth of the 'new economy'. The new urban economies, captured in the global cities of Hong Kong and Singapore, sets in motion, Sassen maintains, a whole series of new dynamics of inequality. As Sassen (1998, p.xxx) notes: 'Major cities have emerged as a strategic site not only for global capital but also for the transnationalization of labor and the formation of transnational identities. In this they are the site for new types of political operations.'

Sassen shows how global cities create a space for the formation of postcolonial discourses characterized by both 'localized cultures' and cosmopolitan elites. As Sassen (1998, p.xxxii) states:

> The space constituted by the global grid of cities, a space with new economic and political potentialities, is perhaps one of the most strategic spaces for the formation of transnational identities and communities ... it is not only the transmigration of capital that takes place in this global grid, but also that of people, both rich (i.e. the new transnational professional workforce) and the poor (i.e. most migrant workers) and it is a space for the transmigration of cultural forms, for the reterritorialization of 'local' subcultures.

Sassen's analysis of, and theoretical engagement with, globalization and transnational processes, highlights the absence of gender in any analysis of these processes. She shows how mainstream accounts of globalization focus on 'abstract economic dynamics and proceed as if these dynamics are inevitably gender neutral' (ibid., p.82). The position taken in this book shows a high level of agreement with Sassen's perspective and purpose in developing a theoretical framework that addresses the intersecting nexus of globalization, social change and gender analysis. As Sassen (1998, p.82) notes: 'The purpose here is to contribute to a feminist analytics that allows us to re-read and reconceptualize major features of today's global economy in a manner that captures strategic instantiations of gendering as well as formal and operational openings that make women visible and lead to greater presence and participation.'

Important questions emerge for gender analysis, and for patterns of inequality, more generally as a result of globalization and its accompanying processes, which include the globalization of labour flows, the growth of global cities, and patterns of corporate restructuring. These include:

- Growing differentiation within the division of labour between, and within gender frameworks.
- Growing 'feminization' of job supply and of business opportunities.
- Increased access to wages and salaries for women at both the upper and lower end of the market.
- Changing gender hierarchies.
- Increased mobility at the high and low end of the job market.

- Increased prominence of women as both visible 'power-brokers' and significant consumers within the global economy.
- Gender and the digital divide.

Gender Inequality in Asian Countries

Globalization and modernization are clearly not gender neutral processes and as Soin (2001, p.5) indicates the question is whether these changes have presented opportunities or risks for women. She notes that despite improvements there still exists significant gender inequality in the Asian region. 'At the heart of most situations adversely affecting the social development prospects of women are strongly prevailing ideologies which lead to a gender gap in employment, education, wages, and access to services' (Soin, 2001, p.6). This is certainly true of the countries in Asia. While some countries in the region including Japan, Singapore, South Korea and Hong Kong are seen as having a high level of social development (see Chapter 1), others, such as China, Vietnam, the Philippines, Thailand and Malaysia are more problematic on issues of gender equality giving rise to considerable disparities regionally.

In the case of China, while the overall level of literacy has risen from 20 percent in 1950 to more than 85 percent at the present time, about 70 percent of all illiterate Chinese are women (*International Herald Tribune*, 2001). The growth of global cities like Shanghai and Beijing is likely to produce disparities within China itself for gender frameworks, leading to a significant urban/rural divide. Despite state intervention in the form of legislation, traditional attitudes are difficult to change. Edwards (2000, p.77) notes that: '... only 11 percent of Beijing women but 69 percent of Tibetan women and 45 percent of Guizhou women fall into this category. Nevertheless even within regions women fare considerably worse than men.' At the other extreme, tertiary institutions frequently have women's studies departments. However as Li Xiaojiang and Zhang Xiaodan (1994) observe: 'Unlike the development of women's studies in the West, the rise of women's studies in China was not the result of a distinct feminist movement ... the discipline of women's studies in contemporary China was initially designed to meditate upon the equality that Chinese women had supposedly achieved according to law established in 1949' (1994, p.140). By contrast the position of women in Vietnam remains a disadvantaged one, the result of a high birth rate, lack of family planning and childcare facilities. As in China there are significant differences between urban and rural life, with rural health and education services having suffered as a result of the market economy and decreased state subsidies.

Filipino women by contrast form a workforce in demand globally. There are five million Filipinos working abroad and most are women. Despite the stereotyped image of migrant women workers, it is estimated that 70 percent of the annual total of seven thousand graduating nurses migrate overseas. Filipino women are well educated by regional standards with high educational status reflected in the fact that

there are more women than men in college and graduate school (Licuanan, 1991) but this does not translate into parity in employment or power in public life. The contribution made by female migrant workers to the economy of the Philippines is being increasingly acknowledged by the government of the Philippines (see Chapter 6).

Despite rapid social change taking place in Thailand, there is still considerable gender inequality in many aspects of life in Thailand. As in China and Vietnam, illiteracy rates remain higher for females than for males at 9 percent for females and 5 percent for males. Soin (2000, p.20) notes that the rapid change from agricultural to an industrial society, together with globalization has been responsible for large numbers of Thai women leaving the countryside to find work in urban areas or overseas. In Thailand, the sex industry and prostitution are seen as employment opportunities for poor and less educated women, and the male tourist revenue generated results in the Thai government's refusal to intervene to either stop prostitution or to legalize it and thus protect the Thai sex-workers. As with other countries in the region, there are stark divisions between urban and rural life in contemporary Malaysia. Female entry to university appears to equal that of males but women account for only two percent of engineering students and only twenty to thirty percent in science, medicine, agriculture and economics.

In countries which show a high level of social development such as Japan and South Korea, ideological factors shape the opportunity structure available to women and define their position in society. In Japan, the constitution makes education a basic right; despite this fewer girls apply for the most competitive schools that will prepare them for university entrance. By the late 1990s only 22.9 percent of university students were women. Most Japanese women get married because of the social pressure but the fertility rate dropped to 1.34 in 2000, below the replacement level of 2.08. The state is encouraging women to have more children and this reinforces the emphasis in Japanese society on women as primarily homemakers.

South Korea is also characterized by the same pervasive traditional ideology of patriarchal Confucianism that pervades the region and despite the 'much vaunted economic miracle of South Korea, this has done little to enlarge the choices of its women who are still constrained by the dictates of Confucianism' (Soin, 2000, p.11). As in Japan, and in most other countries in the region, marriage is a strong expectation in Korea and single women over 30 are frowned upon by society. Despite these social pressures, a growing number of women choose to remain single. About 75 percent of the population in South Korea is urban and according to the Ministry of Finance and Economy nearly 30 percent of women aged 25 to 29 are single, with women heading 16 percent of all families. A state driven rigorous family planning programme has reduced fertility rates to 1.6 live per woman. Despite this, reproduction is still seen as women's primary role, and while education has improved for both genders, women's employment status and career opportunities have remained limited. Soin (2000, p.12) notes that at the tertiary level, education is highly gendered, with women concentrating on education and the humanities and men dominating in science and technology.

The significant socio-economic and gender inequalities apparent in the countries of the region also represent themselves in the increasing 'digital divide' which characterizes a different aspect of gender and inequality. Soin (2000, p.24) frames the debates as follows:

> Rapid scientific progress and diffusion of information and communication technologies (ICT) in industrialized and developing countries over the last decade have led to profound social and economic transformation. One worrying consequence is that the digital divide between the 'information-have' and 'have-nots' has widened ... Despite the growth of the Internet and the explosion of home computer use in wealthier countries, it is estimated that only about five percent of the world's population is connected to the Internet. Most of the 'have-nots' are women, whose access to ICT is limited by lower levels of literacy, fewer economic resources, entrenched gender stereotypes and cultural attitudes.

The 'digital divide' when translated into access and usage of internet technology highlights both regional and gender inequalities. In Singapore, 53 percent of the population is 'on-line' while the figure for Indonesia is 0.7 percent, only 250,000 of the country's 210 million people have internet accounts, the total number of users is 1.5 million. In Malaysia, half of the population (26 million) is rural, but only 1.5 million people (mainly urban) have email access. In Singapore, half of all homes are linked to the Internet, while in South Korea it is just below 40 percent. In terms of gender and the digital divide, most Internet users are men, although in Singapore, 44 percent of Internet users are women, which is slightly higher than in China where women account for 41 percent of internet users.

Globalization, Corporate Restructuring and its Gendered Implications

Sassen (1998) has shown that globalization has created strategic sites where global processes intersect. These processes include: the role of the global information economy, the role of knowledge work, and the functionality of different groups of 'knowledge workers' in this process. Within the global economy, knowledge and knowledge workers (of different types) have become commodities, where 'global talent' competes for scarce and valued resources for example high incomes, status credentials and designer lifestyles. The implications of such global processes has led to changing work identities as the definition of jobs change, and organizations face corporate restructuring to accommodate global changes. Bradley (1993, p.23) raises an important question in the context of women's position within such changes. She asks: Where are the sites where issues around equity and equal opportunities are to be raised with 'an apparent lack of strong and influential advocacy for women in the places where change is being negotiated'? Mackinnon and Brooks (2001, p.7) show that globalization theorists suggest looking beyond specific organizational structures: 'indeed beyond the nation state, to the emerging transnational regimes and institutions. Sassen, for instance, argues that there is an expansion of international civil society, "a contested space", where women can gain visibility as individuals and as collective actors (Sassen, 1998, p.99).' Sassen draws on a global frame of reference to advocate for international law and human rights, however where countries are not signatories to international conventions on human rights, there is little public awareness or debate about the translation of these issues into specific legislation or organizational frameworks. As will be seen in the chapters of this book, the commitment within Hong Kong to legislation in the form of the Bill of Rights Ordinance (1991), and to anti-discrimination legislation, gives women (among others), a strong basis for challenging discriminatory behaviour within an organizational and national context. The climate in Singapore is beginning to change, *The Remaking Singapore Committee* 2002, has put equal opportunities issues on the agenda as the subject of public debate, with some powerful voices emerging from newly appointed women MPs within the Singapore government's own party. This is a big step forward in a country with a tradition of resistance to legislation encompassing anti-discrimination and equal opportunities. It remains to be seen how such debates may be translated into a legislative framework within Singapore.

Differentiation in the Growth of Two Global Cities: Patterns of Migration and Political Change

The emergence of Hong Kong and Singapore as global cities show very different patterns of economic expansion, but somewhat similar patterns of migration. The average annual percentage growth rates of private consumption between 1990-99 was 9.7 percent for Hong Kong and 7.4 percent for Singapore, this compares with 10.2 percent for Taiwan and 12.7 percent for South Korea (Li, 2002). Hong Kong has a very different economic profile from Singapore. Hong Kong is being gradually integrated into the Chinese hinterland economy, with a traditionally laissez-faire and service-based economy. Singapore is a city-state economy, heavily dependent on foreign multi-national capital; it has a free-trade and state-activist tradition. For the economies of Hong Kong and Singapore, the political realities in the late 1940s and early 1950s exerted economic difficulties but the inflow of foreign capital and skilled refugees turned out to be a driving force in the revitalization of the economies.

The emergence of the People's Republic of China (PRC) in 1949 led to large numbers of Chinese migrants moving from Mainland China to Hong Kong between 1948-50. The population of Hong Kong increased by 400 percent between 1945 and 1955. The migrants brought both capital and technical skills and enabled Hong Kong to change from a trading port into an industrial economy. Hong Kong experienced a dip in the growth rate due to the impact of the Cultural Revolution in China in 1996 which, as Li (2002) notes, spilled over into street riots in Hong Kong in 1966-67. The political impact of the uncertainty over the Sino-British Talks on the future of Hong Kong led to a near zero growth rate in 1985 and economic uncertainty in 1995 when the political situation between the Hong Kong Governor Chris Patten and the Chinese authorities over the political reform of Hong Kong reached a crisis point.

Hong Kong also experienced a severe decline in income in 1998 at the peak of the Asian financial crisis.

A significant aspect of Hong Kong's success has been its free market and laissez-faire system. Business has been given maximum freedom and there is little government intervention. The handover to China in 1997 has not changed this economic framework to date. However the emergence of China's special economic zone in the late 1980s led to significant competition and Hong Kong's manufacturing industries lost their cost competitiveness. As Li (2002) notes, the plentiful supply of low cost labour in Southern China attracted Hong Kong industrialists to relocate and establish their bases in China.

In Singapore, there were population movements of mainly ethnic Chinese from Malaysia and Indonesia, but the country was stable. Singapore's process of decolonization did not result in severe destabilization. Singapore successfully achieved full self-government in 1959 and became independent after separating from Malaysia in 1965. As Li (2002) notes, there was no shortage of foreign exchange and investment funds and Singapore's active trade with countries such as Malaysia and Indonesia ensured that the then small city-state economy survived. The population increased by 54 percent to 1,445,900 in 1957. Singapore's economy is clearly subject to changes because of its reliance on global investment and Singaporeans experienced rapid increases in wealth. While the Singapore government was keen on direct intervention, the Hong Kong government pursued a much more indirect approach relying mainly on the private market for development.

Direct foreign investment and the interventionist role of the government in Singapore are two of the major issues in Singapore's experience of economic expansion and growth (see Wong, 1991; Ng and Yang, 1994; Wong and Ng, 1997). Li (2002, p.40) identifies three major factors in Singapore's industrial growth: an open economy, the creation of a growth conducive environment for private enterprise by pursuing macroeconomic policies and investment in public infrastructure and human resources. The level of government intervention in Singapore has been criticized (Young, 1994) by comparison with Hong Kong's laissez-faire approach. In terms of trading partners, by the mid 1990s, China had become Hong Kong's largest trading partner. In Singapore, trade links with ASEAN members are close, although the US and Japan are Singapore's major trading partners. The Cato Institute voted Hong Kong the most open economy in the world for a number of years in the 1990s, while Singapore was in second place.

Both Hong Kong and Singapore have experienced significant political disruptions in their recent histories. The immediate impact of the handover of Hong Kong to China in 1997 led to a number of crises, the fall in property prices in late 1997 and the onset of the Asian financial crisis which resulted in a massive withdrawal of funds and asset depreciation. In addition many Hong Kong citizens emigrated to countries like Canada and Australia resulting in a 'brain-drain' of qualified professionals. Li (2002) notes that surveys have shown that Hong Kong Chinese have a low opinion of political leaders and recent years have shown a vociferous opposition to the current Hong Kong leadership. In Singapore, Li (2002, p.184) comments that Singapore is said 'to be a neo-patrimonial state whereby political leaders and the government bureaucracy act as a father to the citizens ... The welfare of all Singaporeans is given higher priority than the rights of individuals.' Foreign capital is seen as the main engine of society with indigenous capital being small.

Profiles of Political, Economic and Social Change in Hong Kong and Singapore

Hong Kong and Singapore show a number of characteristics of global cities, but also have some unique characteristics in terms of their colonial past, and pivotal position located between Asia and the West, often described as powerhouses of 'Asian capitalism'. The colonial heritage of Hong Kong and Singapore shows an interesting relationship between British hegemony, Asian capitalism and the diasporic Chinese. British hegemonic structures appear in the education, legal and linguistic profiles of Hong Kong and Singapore, particularly in the dominance of English as the medium for business, technology and the media, education, and communication generally. Multi-national companies (MNCs) have been attracted to both Hong Kong and Singapore, by these successful financial centres, Asian capitalist enclaves, and by the predominance of English as the medium of communication.

Singapore has been framed as something of an enigma, being neither Western, nor totally Asian. Whereas Hong Kong had its own indigenous Chinese population, thoroughly colonized by the British, who imposed linguistic and legislative hegemony on Hong Kong, Singapore's tradition was somewhat different. The British established Singapore as a trading station, and turned it into one of the Straits settlements under the control of British India. Initially, the only indigenous population in Singapore were Malays, but Chinese immigrants from various parts of China moved to Singapore to participate in the rapid expansion of trade. As a result of such migration, ethnic Chinese now form the dominant group, and the character, and indeed success of Singapore has been shaped by these diasporic Chinese, who have defined the terms of Asian capitalism in the city-state. Singapore gained self-government in 1959, under the leadership of Lee Kuan Yew, became independent after separating from Malaysia in 1965, and has remained a largely one party state ever since.

Singapore's lack of indigenous authenticity gives rise to significant concerns around national identity, and a great emphasis on the part of the government to create a 'unified nation'. As Ang and Stratton (1995, p.182) observe:

> Economic visibility has always been seen as the *sine qua non* for Singapore's survival. And to a large extent, economic success has become the ideological benchmark for Singapore's *raison d'etre*. However economic success alone is not enough to provide Singapore with the sense of identity which every modern nation-state requires as a vehicle for self-representation. As Stuart Hall has remarked "a nation is not only a political entity but something which produces meaning – *a system of cultural representation*".

This emphasis on creating the idea of a 'nation' has been fraught with tensions and gives Singapore its ambiguous character: 'Singapore, then, is a contradiction in terms: on the one hand its very existence as a modern administrative unit is a thoroughly Western occasion, originating in British colonialism; on the other hand the Republic of Singapore now tries to represent itself as resolutely non-Western by emphasizing its Asianness' (Ang and Stratton, 1995, p.181).

The government of Singapore has at times attempted to engineer a conception of 'Asian values', which frequently get translated into Chinese values, and sit uneasily with Singapore's hybrid culture consisting of Chinese, Malay, Indian and others. This has led to an overemphasis on traditional Confucianist principles. So whereas China and Hong Kong have defined their realities in terms of Communist and now capitalist principles, and have rejected Confucianist principles, the Chinese diasporic elite, now leading Singapore, still draw on a range of Confucianist principles in defining their values. One of the strongest aspects of this has been the attempt by the Singapore government to maintain English as the *lingua franca* of communication, business and technology, while at the same time imposing a rigorous policy of bilingualism through the education system. The rationale for this is set out by Ang and Stratton (1995, p.187):

… while English … is the language of the colonizer, its prominence symbolizes the hegemony of the West, although it is also acknowledged by the leadership … that English is the language of science and technology, so necessary for Singapore's modernization … the Singapore education system has a rigorous policy of bilingualism in place which requires each child to study their ethnic 'mother tongue' – a policy designed to counter the 'negative' effects of English (that is, Westernization), and to inculcate the children with the cultural heritage of their 'race'. The policy of bilingualism, then, is a concrete outcome of Singapore's desire to become modern without becoming Western, to have access to Western science and technology while cultivating 'Asian values'. 'Asian' and 'Western' cultures are portrayed as 'primordial opposites' which are permanently in tension with one another.

Alongside this has been the government's emphasis on the 'Speak Mandarin Campaign' launched in 1979. As Heng and Devan (1995, pp.214-15, n.21) comment:

Singaporeans are commanded by the most prominent slogan in the campaign to "Speak More Mandarin, Less Dialect" [sic], as if Mandarin itself were not a dialect. Mandarin is now referred to as the 'mother tongue' of all Chinese, though virtually all Chinese in Singapore, left to themselves, would likely identify their mother tongues as Teochew, Hokkien, Cantonese, Hainanese, Shanghainese, Hakka, or some other regional dialect spontaneously used in the family. Their official 'mother tongue', by contrast, has to be acquired through formal education … The government has gone to great lengths, nonetheless, to promote Mandarin, including dubbing Cantonese feature films and soap operas from Hong Kong into Mandarin for Singapore television, and instituting a campaign to discourage taxi drivers – notoriously resistant to government regulation

– from speaking in dialect. By the government's own estimate, the measures have been successful: 87 percent of Chinese Singaporeans can now speak Mandarin.

Apart from this engineered form of Singaporean Chineseness, framed within the insistence on Mandarin as 'mother tongue', this is further encapsulated in the reinforcement of Confucian values. Confucianism is expressed in what Heng and Devan (1995, p.203) define as 'the concoction of a "national ideology" grounded in a selective reconfiguration of Confucianism, to promote the interests of the state'. The emphasis on Asian family values, largely defined in Confucianist terms, is translated into gendered inequalities in the workforce in terms of pay, conditions, and in the home where the husband/father ('patriarch') is defined as the provider for the family. It is also reflected in the paternalistic state, dominated by a largely Western educated Chinese elite, who define the terms on which the society should operate. In a powerful discussion of what Heng and Devan (1995, p.207) define as the 'state fatherhood' of the Singaporean state, they maintain that:

> The location of this structure of values in Confucianism, moreover, and the figuration of Confucianism itself as racial and (trans)national identity, continuous with other East Asian societies and with an organically fecund past, stages the modern state and nationalism as merely the theater where a primordial paternal signifier can gather itself new instruments of potency … few nations can boast the degree of thoroughness to which the founders of Singapore have carried the paternal logic of the modern state.

The majority of the Singapore public, particularly the affluent Chinese, has been largely compliant with the dominant regime. However, of late, voices have been raised, particularly from women, and the younger generation, questioning government policy and an opening up of a dialogue is being called for. The future of Singapore offers rich possibilities as Ang and Stratton (1995, p.190) note: 'Situated between the historically privileged discourse of the "West" and the newly powerful and vocal discourse of "Asia", the Singaporean context provides the opportunity for a deconstruction of both these discourses.'

The pattern of traditional Confucian patriarchalism in Singapore is also evident in patterns of marriage, with younger Chinese women marrying much older Chinese men. It is also prevalent in the 'marrying down' phenomenon with well educated men marrying less well educated, and less well positioned women. Despite the fact that the 'marrying down' phenomenon is not prevalent in Hong Kong, with highly educated men tending to marry women of similar educational background, Pearson (1990) shows that girls and boys are still taught to expect that men will assume full responsibility for their families. However women in Hong Kong are encouraged to go onto higher education to gain access to a pool of high status men.

Britain took possession of Hong Kong in 1842, and Hong Kong remained under direct British rule until 1997 when it was 'handed over' to China. Prior to 1997, both the education system and legal system were based on the English system, and English, as in Singapore, remained the language of education, business, and the law. English remains the official language of universities in Hong Kong, except for the Chinese University of Hong Kong, which, Petersen (1998) notes, is considered bilingual. Petersen (1998, p.364) also notes that:

> As a colony, Hong Kong was required to use English as the language of both law and higher education ... Thus until quite recently, the majority of the people of Hong Kong could not read the laws ... a defendant who did not speak English had to rely upon a translator to follow his or her trial. A person was also required to be fluent in English to sit on a jury, making juries unduly representative of expatriates and professionals.

The period of transition since the 'handover' remains unclear on issues of language and education. As regards the law, as Petersen notes, English and Chinese can be used in the legal system and 'Hong Kong is now grappling with the difficult task of how to implement a bilingual legal system' (ibid., p.365). The laws of Hong Kong are now published in both languages and court proceedings can also now be held in Chinese. An article in *The Straits Times* (September 1, 2002) entitled 'Role of English newspapers dwindling in HK', highlights the fact that the government of Hong Kong is now using Chinese newspapers to convey their views to the people of Hong Kong, and English-language newspapers such as the *South China Morning Post*, regarded as the voice of the British colonial government prior to the 1997 handover, are finding themselves without a role and several editors have recently left. In education, universities are increasingly reassessing their position and there is concern about issues of academic freedom, and a greater influence from Beijing, as regards freedom of speech. Petersen (1998, p.340) notes that:

> Officially ... university leaders were appointed in their personal capacities and not as representatives of their institutions, but in reality, their appointments were widely recognized as a process of 'co-option'; a deliberate strategy to reduce resistance among Hong Kong academics and create an impression that the universities supported actions taken by China during the transition.

The position of women in Hong Kong has always been significantly different from Mainland China. There was a Women's Movement in Mainland China during the Nationalist period, which was largely dominated by a Western educated elite and influenced by British and other missionaries, and there was a tradition of women societies and a women's literary tradition (Brooks, 1985). Many women either moved with the Nationalists to Taiwan in 1911, or went on to support the Communist Revolution in 1949. After the Communist Revolution in China (1949), women and the role of the family were the subject of extensive legislative reform, but these reforms did not extend to the women of Hong Kong. In fact women in Hong Kong experienced many of the same patterns of laws and regulations regarding employment as those experienced by women in Britain. Added to these laws were Chinese customary laws, which Britain in the main supported, and which, as will be seen from the chapters of this book, discriminated against women in many respects. Pearson (1990) notes that despite the fact that the United Kingdom is a signatory to the United Nations Convention on the Elimination of All Forms of Discrimination Against Women (1981), which China is also a signatory to, the UK did not extend this convention to Hong Kong. The Civil Service is always a yardstick for how the government of a country discriminates against women, the Civil Service in Hong Kong, as in Britain, took a long time to change and had many discriminatory practices. Pearson (1990, p.124) observes that it was not until 1973 that the government introduced equal pay for female staff, and discontinued the practice of dismissing women on marriage with a gratuity, and then re-employing them on a temporary basis. Until 1981, women civil servants in Hong Kong were not entitled to housing allowances, dental or medical treatment for their families, as their male colleagues in equivalent positions. In Singapore, women civil servants still do not receive the same medical benefits as men. An article in *The Straits Times* (August 24, 2002), entitled 'Women's panel pushes to end discrimination' reports:

> The main point ... made on the civil servants medical benefits is the discrimination in favour of men, allowing them to use up to 60 percent of the $350 annual outpatients subsidy for their dependents. Women cannot. "The treatment towards males and females should be harmonized" ... especially when 54 percent of civil servants, or 33,000, are women. But the government's persistent argument against such a move is that the scheme should reflect Singapore's Asian values, in which men are often responsible for taking care of the family.

Pearson also cites research on attitudes within the Civil Service in Hong Kong, which show negative attitudes towards women in the workplace, shared by men and women. Pearson (1990, p.124) shows that:

> Sixty-eight percent of male respondents but only 65.7 percent of female ones agreed with the statement that women were not inferior to men in their capacity for work. Forty-nine percent of respondents said that they preferred a male supervisor against only 9.5 percent who preferred a female. When asked why, it was found that men were considered to be more decisive, more capable of working under pressure, less emotional, less petty, easier to get along with and easier to communicate with. Females were seen as temperamental, narrow-minded and lacking in potential.

Despite traditional prejudices towards women in leadership from both men and women, there are many examples of highly successful women in Hong Kong. The appointment of women to senior positions in the judiciary and academia is rarer than in the corporate world and in politics. In the corporate world, women occupy prominent positions particularly in family businesses, and many run their own companies. The findings of this research confirm many of the findings of previous research in the area (see Chapter 2). The advances made in Hong Kong through legislation such as the Bill of Rights Ordinance (1991), and the Sex Discrimination Ordinance (1995) has advanced the position of women in Hong Kong as is evidenced in the chapters of this book.

Monitoring Change for Professional Women in Hong Kong and Singapore

Some of the key questions and issues raised by this book include:

- Has globalization and the growth of the global knowledge economy, opened up more opportunities for professional women in organizational life? What are the positives and negatives for women of corporate restructuring, the 'new managerialism', and increased 'flexibility' in organizational structures?
- What impact has organizational and societal change had on professional women?
- To what extent are equal opportunities and anti-discrimination legislation aspects of legislative frameworks in Hong Kong and Singapore?
- To what extent are equal opportunities and equity aspects of social policy debates within Hong Kong and Singapore?
- How do demographic patterns (fertility, marriage patterns, numbers of children, numbers of single versus married women at different ages, numbers of women in workforce) impact on social policy debates, and patterns of social change in Hong Kong and Singapore?
- How significant is the role of foreign migrant labour in serving the needs of advanced economies? To what extent are opportunities for professional women facilitated by the employment of foreign migrant labour in Hong Kong and Singapore? To what extent does the employment of foreign migrant labour offset the need for organizations to provide childcare facilities and become 'family-friendly firms'?
- To what extent are women still confronted by organizational constraints and barriers in terms of career opportunities? Are organizations still characterized by 'cultures of masculinity' (Collinson and Hearn, 1996; Prichard, 2000)?
- What issues exist around leadership and management for professional women in organizations, and what organizational styles are still the preferred or dominant ones in organizations? To what extent are women leaders and managers acceptable within organizational cultures, and as acceptable to male and female employees?
- What personal and social issues confront professional women in senior positions? What are some of the issues raised for professional women around being single, marriage and family obligations, spousal attitudes to career, parenting /care giving and household, attitudes to spouse/partner's career, support structures in the home to assist women in their career.
- What organizational factors can be identified as advancing the position of women in leadership and management? What global factors can be identified as advancing the position of women in leadership and management?

Conclusion

The chapters of this book examine these, and other, issues within the context of globalization and changing professional work cultures in Asia. Theoretical debates around globalization are combined with empirical research on professional women in two global cities, Hong Kong and Singapore. This book presents empirical research on professional women in academic and corporate life within the context of the growth of the new economy. More broadly the book focuses on the intersection of globalization, gender and the new economy and assesses the impact of the changes for professional work cultures and more specifically the impact on women professionals in specific work contexts located within two Asian global cities, which present a specific site for the intersecting nexus of globalization, gender and social change.

Chapter 1

Globalization, Gender and Changing Work Cultures in Asia

This chapter explores the impact of globalization on gender, and changing work cultures in Asia. The chapter examines the impact of globalization, the growth of the new economy, and its impact on professional women, in the context of organizational and societal change in two global cities in the region, Hong Kong and Singapore. The first section of the chapter frames the theoretical debates, and explores the issues around globalization and socio-economic change and examines the relationship between globalization, and changing work cultures. It also considers the relationship between globalization, gender and labour market segmentation. More specifically this first section of the chapter explores the impact of globalization in the context of Southeast Asia more broadly, and considers issues of transnationalism, gender and the 'feminization' of labour regimes in the region. The relationship between globalization and transnational labour migration is considered, and the 'feminization' of transnational labour migration is seen as highly significant in the region. The implications of such trends are investigated in the specific contexts of the global cities of Hong Kong and Singapore. The second section of the chapter examines the relationship between globalization, the global knowledge economy, and organizational change and considers the gendered implications of these changes. The third section considers more specific economic and social change in Hong Kong and Singapore, particularly as it impacts on professional women. Both Singapore and Hong Kong, while very different, see themselves as highly significant centers for the region in a number of ways. Both can be defined as 'global cities'. Both have positioned themselves as 'market leaders' in terms of the 'new economies', and as 'global knowledge hubs' for the growth of the global knowledge economy. Both centers are experiencing rapid economic, social, and political change and dealing with organizational change, and changing work cultures and identities. This chapter examines some of the theoretical underpinnings of the debates around globalization, gender and social change, and considers the particular interpolation of the debates in the context of Hong Kong and Singapore.

Globalization, Transnationalism and Changing Work Cultures

Globalization has become a valuable theoretical framework for investigating some key global and national issues in understanding socio-economic change. What becomes apparent is that national economies are less and less a unitary category in the face of new forms of globalization (Sassen, 1998), and that globalization can allow us to understand the ways in which the global information economy is embedded in local economies and work cultures, and shows the micro processes within localized economies through which globalization exists. However, Sassen notes that mainstream accounts of economic globalization is often confined to a very narrow economistic profile centered on a range of narratives 'enacted, constituted, and legitimized by men and /or in male gendered terms' (Sassen, 1998, p.82).

The dominance of world markets has produced global cities whose orientation to world markets has frequently raised questions about the relationship of such global cities with their nation-states and their regions. Singapore and Hong Kong are both global cities but occupy unique relationships in relation to larger economic and social structures, and to their regional location. Singapore is both a global city with a global and international outreach in terms of world markets; and it is also a nation-state occupying a unique position in the region. Similarly Hong Kong is also a global city, but also a Special Administrative Region of China, and thus also occupies a unique position in relation to its regional location.

The emergence of global cities has proved to be 'a strategic site not only for global capital but also for the transnationalization of labor and the formation of transnational identities ...' (Sassen, 1998, p.xxx). Such sites offer new economic and political potentialities in the creation of both transnational identities and communities, such communities consist of both the rich, in the form of the new transnational professional workforce, and the poor, in the form of migrant (increasingly female) workers. There are significant social and political implications of the transnationalization of labour, and, as Sassen notes, there has been a failure to create new forms and regimes to encompass these new identities and formations for those who 'do not regard the nation as their sole or principal source of identification ...' (ibid.).

Theorizing Globalization as a 'Cultural Process'

The theorizing of globalization has been decidedly silent on the issue of gender and some theorists of globalization do not deal with gender at all in their major theoretical contribution to the debate on 'global modernities' (Featherstone, Lash and Robertson, 1995). There is a lack of agreement among writers about the 'periodization of globalization'. Robertson (1987) maintains that the uniformity created by globalization in terms of the control of information and capital produces a single social and cultural space. This overarching process of control, which defines the nature of social relations over time and space, can be seen as having precedence over the concepts of 'nation' and 'society'. This model of globalization is one that 'sees it as an epoch contemporaneous with postmodernity' (Stivens, 2000, p.28N). This is a position shared by Harvey (1989) and Lash and Urry (1994).

While the cultural theorists' model of globalization (Robertson, 1992; Turner, 1990) has moved the debate away from a crude preoccupation with the economic, it is a model which does not address the issue of gender. As Stivens (2000, p.10) observes: 'In order to theorize the global dimensions of culture and society, it is necessary to investigate the interrelations of public and private, of the economy and the domestic, of male and female roles, and of ideologies of work and politics and ideologies of gender.' It is here that the work of Saskia Sassen (1996) is so relevant to the debates around globalization, particularly her point that as politics becomes more global, human rights become increasingly part of its normative regulation (Sassen, 1996, pp.35-6). This view is shared by those theorists (Ghai, 1999) who argue that the increasing power of corporations resulting from globalization erodes the rights of others. As Stivens (2000, p.12) notes this position receives support from the literature on transnational labour migration (see Ghai, 1999). Sassen (1996, p.88) raises the question of what institution is going to enforce human rights in this new globalized world? Stivens (2000, p.12) also raises the question that: 'Given the masculinism of existing international structures, how would women's interests be promoted within such new orders?' Sassen's work is particularly valuable in raising both macro and micro dimensions underpinning the relationship between globalization, gender, and social change.

Globalization, Gender and Labour Market Segmentation

Globalization not only provides a valuable theoretical framework, but it is also provides a way of understanding the process of restructuring the global market economy. As Sassen (1998, p.90) shows, globalization has resulted in the formation of new types of labor-market segmentation that highlight 'strategic instantiations of gendering in the global economy'. In this process she says that two characteristics stand out:

- One is the weakening of the firm in structuring the employment relation which leaves more to the market.
- A second form of restructuring of the labor market is what can be described as the shift of labor-market functions to the household or community.

Sassen goes on to note that both of these trends highlight some very negative aspects of restructuring in relation to labour markets, including 'a devaluing of jobs (from full to part-time jobs, from jobs offering upward mobility within firms to dead end jobs ...) and a feminization of employment in these jobs' (Sassen, 1998, p.90). An integral dimension within this relationship between globalization and corporate restructuring has been the 'transmigration of labour', which has also been shown to be a significantly gendered process:

> The expansion of the high-income workforce in conjunction with the emergence of new cultural forms has led to a process of high-income gentrification that rests, in the last analysis, on the availability of a vast supply of low-wage workers ... the immigrant woman serving the white middle class professional woman has replaced the traditional image of the black female servant serving the white master (Sassen, 1998, p.91).

The labour intensive nature of 'high-income gentrification' is an important aspect of the emergence of global cities, and the demographics and patterns of migration entailed in this process. It is a pattern that characterizes many of the global cities of Southeast Asia and is certainly a prominent aspect of the work culture(s) of Singapore and Hong Kong. As Sassen (1998, p.122) notes:

> High income gentrification replaces much of this capital intensity with workers directly and indirectly. Behind the gourmet food stores and speciality boutiques that have replaced the self-service supermarket and department store lies a very different organization of work. Similarly, high-income residences in the city depend to a much larger extent on hired maintenance staff than the middle class suburban home.

Globalization thus has a number of ramifications for gender at both ends of the labour market. In addition to the transmigration of (largely female) labour market serving the needs of global cities, at the high income professional end of the market, particularly in the context of corporate restructuring and organizational change, we see an expansion in the number of professional women holding senior positions. This is partly the result of the growing transnational professional labour market, and partly the growing feminization of job supply, and the growing feminization of management, often the indirect result of the global knowledge economy, which has had a significant impact on gender hierarchies in many areas of work.

Globalization and Southeast Asia

The relationship between transnationality, global capital, and the feminization of labour is a particularly interesting one in the context of Southeast Asia. As Ong notes, '… in Asia, transnational flows and networks have been the key dynamics in shaping cultural practices, the formation of identity, and shifts in state strategies' (Ong, 1999, p.17). Transnationalism takes on a particular inflection in the context of the so-called Asian tiger economies, given the history of diasporan trading groups such as the ethnic Chinese, who play a major role in relation to transnational Asian capitalism. As Ong states: 'Global capitalism in Asia is linked to new cultural representations of "Chineseness" … in relation to transnational Asian capitalism … The changing status of diasporan Chinese is historically intertwined with the operations and globalizations of capital' (Ong, 1999, p.7). These aspects of transnationalism have clear implications for the economies, work cultures and organizations of Hong Kong and Singapore.

Diasporic Chinese within the region have played and are playing a key role in the emergence of a 'new flexible' capitalism in the region. In addition as Ong (1999, p.35) argues:

> Many formerly colonized countries in Southeast Asia are themselves emergent capitalist powerhouses that are 'colonizing' territories and peoples in their backyard or further afield: Indonesia has invaded and colonized East Timor, while Malaysian, Singaporean, and Hong Kong entrepreneurs are factory managers in China, timber barons in New Guinea

and Guyana, and hotel operators in England and the United States. These strategies of economic colonization by countries formerly colonized by the West represent new forms of engaging dissent at home and capital abroad.

Women, Labour Migration and 'Flexible Accumulation'

In framing the debate around 'flexible accumulation', Nonini and Ong (1997, p.9) maintain that a 'constellation of technical, financial and institutional innovations that have occurred since the early 1970s has led to a shift in late capitalism from mass industrial production to globalized regimes of flexible accumulation (Harvey, 1989)'. Drawing on the work of David Harvey (1989, p.147), Nonini and Ong point out that flexible accumulation: '...rests on flexibility with respect to labor processes, labor markets, products, and patterns of consumption. It is characterized by the emergence of entirely new sectors of production, new ways of providing financial services, new markets, and, above all, greatly intensified rates of commercial, technological, and organizational innovation.' As Nonini and Ong go on to show, intrinsic to these changes are the mobility of peoples, commodities, ideas and capital on a global scale. As they note: 'We can thus speak of the simultaneous implosion of space and the speed up of all aspects of economic (and hence cultural) life, in this latest episode of what Harvey (1989) refers to as "time-space compression"' (Nonini and Ong, 1997, p.10).

Two major implications have emerged from these developments, the first is the formation of new kinds of social organization, which are de-territorialized and flexible. As Nonini and Ong have observed: 'Labor markets have been reorganized by new forms of labor regulation ... processes have been increasingly segmented, deskilled, and globalized into a new international division of labor increasingly independent of specific places and their populations across the world. At the same time, a proliferation and segmentation of new commodity markets of global scope have promoted and in turn been fed by new lifestyle consumer constituencies' (ibid). These changes have not necessarily been positive in terms of the establishment of new work cultures and relationships, as Nonini and Ong observe: 'Older asymmetrical power relationships are reinforced, while new ones have emerged. Women, in particular, young women, have become the largest section of local populations to be drafted as temporary, contingent, and part-time laborers for industrial subcontractors and other firms using the forms of labor regulation characterizing flexible accumulation (Ong, 1991)' (ibid). The reorganization of both labour markets and forms of social organization characterized by flexibility and mobility, combined with the formation of new commodity driven consumer markets, is a feature of both Hong Kong and Singapore.

The growth of Asian capitalism has been the subject of considerable tension particularly from moderate and radical Islamist groups, the former who promote a counter discourse around a new Islam, friendly to capitalism, typical of the pronouncements of Malaysia's Dr Mahathir Mohammed. The latter have more recently been associated with radical Islamist terrorist cells that pose threats to the traditionally stable economic basis of the region. The impact of the latter groups for countries like Singapore and the wider region is as yet unknown (Brooks, 2003). At the opening of the Singapore Parliament (March 2002), the President posed the dual problems of globalization and regional threats to peace from radical Islamization in the following way. On the issue of globalization he noted that other countries in the region including Japan, Korea, Taiwan and Hong Kong are all pursuing the same opportunities around the development of the global knowledge economy. In addition on the subject of the threat posed by the spread of Islamization he commented: '... the spread of narrow, radical interpretations of Islam in the countries around us, influenced by the world-wide tide of Islamic fundamentalism, will have its effect ... A troubled region and an Asean preoccupied with internal problems, mean fewer growth opportunities for Singapore in the region' (*The Straits Times*, 2002, p.H2).

Globalization and the 'Feminization' of Transnational Labour Migration

The current process of globalization has impacted on patterns and processes of transnational labour migration (Sassen, 1988) and has more recently led to the increasing 'feminization' of transnational labour migration. Tyner (2001) shows that the countries of Southeast Asia, particularly South Korea, Singapore and Taiwan have become important sites of both capital accumulation and labour in-migration. Tyner also notes that the volume of migration has both increased and become more diversified and in the process he notes the increasing feminization of transnational migration (Tyner, 2001; Heyzer, 1989; Zlotnik, 1995). Robinson also notes that mobility in the global economy was predominantly male until recently with the increasing demand for women domestic workers and the growth of international trade in sex workers (Robinson, 2001).

> In the Philippines ... which is the world's largest exporter of government sponsored contract labor migration over 55 percent of all migrant workers are women (Tyner, 2000a). Reflecting the pervasiveness of gendered stereotypes and the international division of labor, the increase in woman migrants is accounted for by the observation that migrant women are usually concentrated in certain occupations including domestic services, entertainment and health care services (Cheng, 1996, p.139). Hong Kong, Singapore, Taiwan, and Malaysia, have emerged as key destinations for female foreign domestic workers (Cheng, 1996; Huang and Yeoh, 1996; Wong, 1996; Chin, 1997) (Tyner, 2001, p.2).

The state frequently intervenes in these instances to control the market when it comes to migrant labour. Christine Chin's analysis of domestic service in Malaysia shows that it cannot be regarded as simply the movement of women from countries where there is a labour surplus such as Indonesia and the Philippines, to areas where there is a labour shortage. As Chin (1998) notes the state regulates the flow in important ways through controlling the factors such as religion and cost. For example the state in Malaysia insists that Muslim families have Muslim, usually cheaper, servants from Indonesia, while the Chinese have Christian, and generally more expensive, domestic servants. As Robinson notes: '… government policy is important in regulating migrant flow in a manner which serves the imperative of the creation of a Malay middle class to counter the economic and social power of the Chinese' (Robinson, 2001, p.6).

In Singapore, as Heng observes, the Singaporean state, as with many other countries in the region, also profits from the 'expropriation of female domestic labour that is commonly left outside the purview of protective employment legislation. Singapore, for example, extracts a maid "levy" from the employers of domestic workers (since April 1991, S$300 per worker), a sum that is often greater than the wages the workers earn themselves. The Singapore government reaps S$234 million annually from the maid levy (Heyzer and Wee, 1992), and a massive S$1.3 billion in 1992 from all foreign-workers levies' (Heng, 1997, p.32).

The Role of Female Migrant Labour in Serving the Needs of Advanced Economies

Globalization has been central in facilitating the movement of capital, commodities and labour. Earlier phases of globalization emphasized the movement of capital and commodities but as Tyner (2001, p.2) notes: '… the current phase of economic restructuring is broadly characterized by new centres of capital accumulation and an increasingly differentiated division of labour on the basis of ethnicity, gender and geography.' As Basch et al. (1994, p.24) contend: '… current transnationalism marks a new type of migrant experience, reflecting an increased and more pervasive global penetration of capital.' The implications of these flows of migrant labour, particularly female migrant labour to work as domestic servants, have meant that professional women gain greater freedom. Lee (1996, p.11) notes that: 'It is indeed ironic that the economic attainments of many women in host countries (for example women professionals in the United States, Canada … and Singapore) have come about through the incorporation of women migrants of minority races as domestic servants and childcare providers.'

The governments of Hong Kong and Singapore have adopted an open-door policy with regard to female migrant domestic labour. As Tam (1999, p.264) notes: 'The prevalence of employment of foreign domestic helpers reflects the assumption behind social policy making that provision of childcare remains the responsibility of the private domain.' The current policy on foreign domestic labour in Hong Kong puts no ceiling on the number of such work visas, and figures from the Census and Statistics Department in Hong Kong for 1997, show that over 110,000 families, that is, 6.1 percent of all domestic households, employ one or more overseas domestic workers to assist with housework and childcare. Tam (1999, p.265) reports that: 'About 71 percent of the households who employ live-in helpers have children below the age of 12.'

There is no specific ordinance covering the employment of foreign domestic workers in Hong Kong (unlike Singapore) and in theory they work under the same employment ordinances as local workers, including protection of wages, regulation of gender conditions of employment and employee compensation. However the position of the foreign domestic labourer is, as Tam notes: '... vulnerable to discrimination because of their non-citizen status, gender, occupation and income level, as well as employment and visa conditions under which they were allowed to enter' (Tam, 1999, p.264).

Singapore, like Hong Kong has a history of waged domestic service (Wong, 1996). The rapid transformation of Singapore's economy involved 'the massive mobilization of young women on a scale never before experienced in the country' (Heyzer, 1986, p.47). As Wong notes by the end of the 1970s, the hitherto ready supply of domestic servants from the ranks of the working class had come to an end. In addition women were no longer withdrawing from the labour market after marriage, thus creating an additional demand for domestic labour. The employment of foreign domestic labourers in Singapore began in the 1960s, particularly from Malaysia and Indonesia. By the late 1970s, foreign domestic labour from the Philippines began to develop. As Wong (1996, p.92) notes:

> ... the genesis of the Filipino entry into the Singaporean domestic labor market can be traced back to the contacts made by Singaporean male tourists to Manila, then the sex tourist capital of Southeast Asia, in the second half of the seventies. Such men were often self-employed taxi-drivers or hawkers. As small-time businessmen, they saw the opportunity to marry business with pleasure by bringing some girls back with them to Singapore for placement on the domestic labor market. When booked under the Employment Agency Act (enacted in 1958 and amended only in 1984), offenders were fined and given an application form to file for a license as an employment agency. By the early eighties, more serious and respectable recruiters had identified the new market niche which had emerged in the labor market and were diversifying sources of supply.

The Foreign Maids Scheme was introduced into Singapore in 1978. Under this scheme, as Wong notes: '... domestic workers from "non-traditional" sources ... the Philippines, Indonesia, Thailand, India, Sri Lanka, Bangladesh and Myanmar ... are covered by the Employment Act.' By the end of the 1990s in Singapore, Yeoh, Huang and Gonzalez (1999) maintain that there was one foreign maid for every eight households. Lyons (2004) citing slightly later figures, states that there is estimated to be 140,000 foreign domestic workers in Singapore which equates with one foreign domestic worker to every seven households (Huang and Yeoh, 2003). Toh and Tay (1996), in commenting on the situation in Singapore, conclude that there is a dependency on maids and the maid culture has become a way of life.

The situation regarding protection of foreign domestic workers remains unsatisfactory with a high level of maid abuse in Singapore and little real protection for these workers. In comparing the position of migrant domestic workers in Hong Kong, Singapore and Taiwan, Cheng (1996) maintains that Hong Kong has the most progressive system for the protection of migrant domestic workers (Alcid, 1994, pp.170-75). Both local and migrant domestic workers are protected by the labour law. The Employment Ordinance provides the minimum protection to these women workers in regard to their employment terms and working conditions. Cheng (1996, p.16) notes that: 'Migrant domestic workers are more vulnerable both in Taiwan and Singapore due to the lack of legal protection, the denial of access to the redress system, the inadequacy of the legal infrastructure, the transfer of power from state to private individuals, intrusive immigration regulations and the limited function of the NGO community.'

In these two countries, local and migrant domestic workers are excluded from the protection of labour legislation. In addition to the lack of basic employment protection in Hong Kong, Singapore and Taiwan, Cheng notes that migrant domestic workers are subject to restrictive immigration regulations. One regulation that serves as a disincentive to the pursuit of their legal rights is the restriction on employment during legal proceedings. Migrant women are not allowed to work when they have cases in court. In addition in Singapore and Taiwan: '... the governments further adopt intrusive immigration regulations that constitute gender discrimination. In both countries migrant women domestic workers have to go through pregnancy tests every six months and they are subject to immediate deportation if found pregnant' (Cheng, 1996, p.117).

The influx of foreign domestic laborers into Hong Kong and Singapore has provided invaluable support to increasing the participation in the labour force of women of childbearing age. As Ngo (1992) shows, the increasing participation of women in the paid workforce, has, in part, facilitated the economic success of Hong Kong in the last few decades. A similar pattern can be seen in Singapore. Yet foreign migrant domestic workers remain susceptible to discrimination and abuse, as is very clear with the recent cases of abuse and murder of foreign maids in Singapore. The situation is unlikely to change given the lack of a legislative framework to protect foreign domestic workers rights.

Globalization, Gender Ideology and Gender Sensitivity Indicators

According to the United Nations Human Development Report 2000, Japan, Singapore, Hong Kong, South Korea and Brunei are categorized as having achieved high human development. The Human Development Report, 1995, concludes: 'In no society do women enjoy the same opportunities as men. In all countries the GDI (Gender-Sensitive Development Index) is lower than the HDI (Human Development Index), reflecting lower achievements for women than for men. Gender gaps in education and health are closing but opportunities for economic and political participation are still limited for women.' There is a significant gap in countries in the region between the HDI and GDI and gender ideology. As Soin (2001) notes, many of the countries in the region are 'authoritarian democracies' and 'the nationalist agenda is characterized by paternalistic and patriarchal beliefs that overshadow the gender agenda.' However increasing globalization and urbanization have created a demand for more women to enter the labour force. 'Also the pressures of maintaining a middle class way of life have forced more married women to seek paid employment. In Southeast Asia and Hong Kong most middle class families employ maids or domestic help and this has hindered and postponed some of the negotiations over changing roles and responsibilities within the household' (Soin, 2001, p.7).

Other social and demographic patterns to emerge include marriage choices. Women are marrying later in Singapore and households are shrinking in size, and in Hong Kong, women head more than 20 percent of households ... in addition among older persons more women than men are not married. In Singapore the government operates to manage and control economic and social strategy including acting to manage fertility through a selectively pro-natalist population policy. Its attitude to gender ideology remains resolutely disengaged with its recent rejection of a call for the introduction of an equal opportunities policy. As Soin (2001, p.14) notes:

> With modernization, the numbers of educated women remaining single are rising in Singapore, as in other countries. However, the policy makers regard these educated women who reject marriage as socially unacceptable because they are not fulfilling the national objective of reproducing 'quality' population. One of the unwritten penalties for these highly educated single women is that they are perceived as unsuitable for political candidacy. Census 2000 highlighted two groups of people with the highest number of singles – well educated women and less educated men. Women with less than secondary education are two or three times more likely to marry than those with university degrees, while one in four female graduates is married to a non-graduate. Government sponsored matchmaking units have been established to help singles meet suitable partners.

Patterns of literacy and higher education in Singapore are very high indeed and apart from certain anomalies women have nearly equal access to education. In Singapore 44 percent of Internet users are women, slightly higher than in China where women account for 41 percent.

Globalization and the Global Knowledge Economy: Gendered Implications for the 'New Economies'

The emergence of global cities such as London, Tokyo, Hong Kong and Singapore highlights one of the central features of the globalization process, a highly differentiated workforce, divided between elite knowledge workers and low-paid service workers who provide the personal services that they demand. Thurow (2000, p.21) maintains that the knowledge-based economy is transforming the role of the state so that: '... instead of being a controller of economic events within its borders, the nation-state is increasingly having to become a platform-builder to attract global economic activity to locate within its borders.'

This systematic shift towards the centrality of knowledge in economic development has been best captured by Manuel Castells. Castells (1998, p.345) argues that a new informational/global economy has emerged in which 'knowledge and information are the essential materials of the new production process, and education is the key quality of labour', so that: '... the new producers of informational capitalism are the knowledge generators and information processors whose contribution is most valuable to the firm, the region, and the national economy.'

The familiarly known 'tiger' economies of Hong Kong, Singapore, Taiwan and South Korea were all receptive to the impact of globalization and the global knowledge economy. They had relatively little in the way of natural resources on which to base their development, particularly so for Hong Kong and Singapore. Thus the main assets that they had available were the energies and skills of their people. By 1960, all four countries had educational attainment measured in average years of schooling in the population over fifteen, which was substantially above other developing countries and closer to that of OECD nations. By 1990, the OECD average of 9.02 years had been overtaken by Hong Kong (9.15 years) and South Korea (9.94 years), while Taiwan (7.98 years) and Singapore (5.89 years) lagged somewhat behind, but still substantially ahead of South Asia (3.85 years) (Green et al., 1999). Green et al., further note that states such as Singapore, South Korea and Taiwan intervened in their educational systems in such a way as to make crucially important contributions to successful economic growth. These Asian tiger economies led by Malaysia, Hong Kong and Singapore saw in the global knowledge economy the ability to 'transform their economies through "techno-preneurship and e-business, taking advantage of the Internet opportunity to skip a generation of catch-up with the West"' (*The Economist*, February 5, 2000, p.64).

Hong Kong has been slower than Singapore and Malaysia in intervening in, and restructuring the economy with the aim of fostering the transition to an information and technology-intensive economic pattern. However in the last few years the pace has picked up and in a 1999 Policy Address the objective for Hong Kong was to become 'a world class city' which was not only a major Chinese city but also the 'most cosmopolitan in Asia'. To achieve this Hong Kong would have to 'turn increasingly to innovative knowledge-intensive economic activities, make the best use of information technology' and restructure the economy with this as the goal. Alongside this emphasis has been an immigration policy designed to attract 'designer immigrants' with skills and talents that could contribute to this economy. The Commission on Innovation and Technology argued that a 'liberal immigration policy to attract talents is a common thread among many successful economies in the world'. In support of this suggestion it was stated that: 'In the knowledge-based economy, intellectual capital is a factor of production as important as, if not more important than financial capital. Bringing in additional intellectual capital would boost economic growth and employment in the same way as external financial capital contributes to the economy.' The Commission went on to say that in order to 'jump-start the development of higher value and more technology-intensive economic activities, Hong Kong must attract talents from other places to augment its intellectual capital quickly' (www.info.gov.hk). Similar issues have emerged in Singapore particularly around the 'Remaking Singapore Policy Debate' (2002). The implications of these policy debates are significant for immigration policy, for the nature of employment and for education, particularly tertiary education, and are central to the growth of the global knowledge economy.

So what are some of the gendered implications of the growth of the global knowledge economy? This has been explored by Brooks and Mackinnon (2001) who note that central to international competitiveness and to any definition of 'entrepreneurial' are the components of the technology revolution: information technology (IT), artificial intelligence (AI), advanced telecommunications and biotechnology. As Kelves and Hood (1992) state: '... technology is at once science and product. It collapses the distinction between knowledge and commodity, knowledge becomes technology' (cited in Slaughter and Leslie, 1997, p.38). As Mackinnon and Brooks (ibid.) continue, not only does the focus on technoscience have gendered implications in that women are less likely to be involved in those areas, but the concomitant time-space compression that IT fosters (Harvey, 1993) has a different impact on the lives of men and women. The need to 'master-mind the volatility', in Harvey's terms to be 'highly adaptable and fast-moving in response to market shifts' (1993, p.287), has differing resonances for those whose predominant location is in the more reflective areas and those who can heed the market's call. As Brooks and McKinnon note (2001, pp.3-4):

> Increasingly innovation is seen as a driver for economic growth in Organization for Economic Cooperation and Development (OECD) countries wishing to guarantee highly paid jobs (Marceau, 2000). 'Innovation and high levels of technology are more important as competitive weapons in knowledge intensive industries but are increasingly important to the success of all industries', claims Marceau (p.217). The urgent need for innovation and the knowledge underpinning innovation is at the base of the idea of a learning economy, she argues. And what is the basis of support for a learning economy? Marceau claims it is one 'where organizations collaborate at least as much as they compete' (p.219) ... it is to the universities that we must look for innovation. But although lip service is paid to collaboration, in practice the chase for funds and the system of promotion and reward rest on a highly competitive system, and one becoming increasingly so. In this intensely competitive world, attempts to collaborate to gain competitive advantage are fraught with tension.

We have already seen how significantly globalization has impacted on Southeast Asia in terms of the growth of the 'new economies' and the focus of the region on the growth of the global knowledge economy. The incisive impact of the Asian 'tiger economies' defined the terms of reference of the new economies and set the agenda for the rapid emergence of the global knowledge economy driven by the new technologies and the 'new entrepreneurialism'.

Economic and Social Change in Hong Kong and Singapore

Both Singapore and Hong Kong, while very different, see themselves as highly significant centers for Asia in a number of ways. Both have positioned themselves as 'market leaders' in technological and economic growth and in the way they are addressing the global knowledge economy. Both centers are experiencing rapid economic and social change and both are more recently dealing with the economic downturn, recession and retrenchment. Both Singapore and Hong Kong are dealing with the influx of large migrant female populations and this in itself is giving rise to significant social issues in both locations.

There are significant implications of the recent economic downturn in the region as a whole and the growth in unemployment in both Hong Kong and Singapore. Inevitably the backlash of the economic recession is directed at women. A number of articles in the media show how these trends are manifesting themselves. An article in *The Straits Times* (December 14, 2001) entitled 'HK men fear losing out to women in workplace' outlines how Hong Kong men are fearful that they are losing out to women in the workplace, especially single women who are devoted to their careers. 'Economic hard times combined with a reversal in the territory's gender ratio have made the issue the talk of the town. There are 1,000 females to every 960 males, compared with 1,000 females per 1,038 males a decade ago.'

Local newspapers analyze how women are faring in what has become an increasingly fierce competition for men. They carry articles about why Hong Kong men seem to prefer marrying more traditional mainland Chinese women and how women should lower their expectations for marriage partners. Not only is there an emphasis on the numbers of successful single women, remaining single, but the stories also focus on how some female professionals make more money than their male counterparts. As Sociology Professor Odalia Wong, from the Hong Kong Baptist University comments: '… in an economic downturn, people look for people to blame … Women have become the scapegoats.' The number of Hong Kong women who remain single into their 30s and 40s has been rising for 15 years. The percentage who have never married hit a new high of nearly 17 percent last year. This compares with an increase of single men in the same age bracket to 21 percent. As is the case with Singapore, the single professional women phenomenon is seen as deviant or a social problem. Research shows that higher education levels among women have put more into professional jobs, making them financially independent. Many postpone or even give up the idea of marrying. As Hong Kong Polytechnic lecturer Catherine Ng, who is 41 and unmarried, states: 'Women's level of education and economic power is much higher than in the old days. Our confidence has gone up and we're not so willing to compromise.'

In another article from Hong Kong in *The Straits Times* (March 5, 2002) entitled 'Executives suffer rapes in silence to keep their jobs', women executives in Hong Kong are keeping silent about sexual harassment and rape in the workplace for fear of losing their jobs in the midst of an economic recession. The Association Concerning Sexual Violence Against Women revealed that there had been a five-fold increase in the number of calls for help made by women executives. The association went on to say that of the 16 calls made by women executives last year some had been from senior executives and managers, this was reported in the *Apple Daily*. The article stated that 'many women who were sexually violated by their bosses or superiors were forced to suffer their humiliation in silence because they risked losing their jobs if they kicked up a fuss about it', a director of the association is quoted as saying. It was also revealed that the association received 1,700 calls last year, including 200 from rape victims. About 30 percent of the victims are believed to have known their attackers.

Women in Singapore have not made the significant advances that women in Hong Kong have made and lack the legislative framework which women in Hong Kong have available. Anti-discrimination legislation in the form of the Bill of Rights Ordinance (1991) and Sex Discrimination Ordinance (1995) in Hong Kong, allows women to test issues of discrimination in the courts. Legislation of this type does not exist in Singapore. This has resulted in significant gender inequalities in many areas of work including the Civil Service, academia and business. In Singapore only 6 in 100 listed firms' directors are women, way behind the US, which stands at 12 percent. An article in *The Business Times (Singapore)* (March 16-17, 2002) by Catherine Ong reports that the number of women listed on the main boards of companies was a mere 6.1 percent. 'There were 227 female directors out of a total of 3,727 directors, according to figures obtained from the latest available annual reports, company disclosures and SGX ... These figures lag those in other developed countries like the US, Australia and Canada where female directors account for 12.4 percent, 10.7 percent and 9.1 percent respectively.' The article goes on to raise the question of whether there is equal opportunity and equal access for the majority of the population, and the consequences for an open economy like Singapore, '... if the best and brightest are, by choice or custom, kept outside of mainstream business. Women account for 50.04 percent of the population and 39.6 percent of the labour force of 2.12 million. They are among the best educated, comprising 11 percent of the 1.19 million economically active persons last year with degrees and diploma qualifications, against 16.4 percent for males.' The article quotes a former woman cabinet minister who states: 'There's a glass ceiling whoever you look at it whether in politics, in business, in Asia, in the US. Let's not pretend there's equal opportunity ... Look at the government, last year was the first time they've put 20 women MPs up for election, yet they put no women in the cabinet.' Other women directors interviewed for the article blamed 'the old boy network' for the exclusion of many capable women from boardrooms. 'The director recruitment process, women said, is in practice an internal referral system, notwithstanding the presence of nominating committees in some companies.' The Singapore Institute of Directors commented: 'I don't think there's a deliberate attempt to keep women from getting onto boards. Historically, there aren't too many women in senior corporate positions. Many women don't continue with their careers after they've a family.' Statistics show this comment to be wholly inaccurate. A further article on women in the boardroom in Singapore also by Ong indicated that the majority of women directors appeared to have been appointed through family connections. The International Women's Forum in Singapore has started a register of women who have the potential to take on corporate directorships with a view to making them known to corporations on the lookout for board members.

Conclusion

This chapter has explored the intersecting nexus of globalization, gender and changing labour markets. The theoretical underpinnings of the debates around globalization and socio-economic change in Southeast Asia have been considered, as well as the implications of the growth of the new economies for the global knowledge hubs of Hong Kong and Singapore. What is clear from the theoretical debates is that globalization is creating uniformity in the patterning of different categories of worker and work culture, frequently clustered around the new global cities, of which Hong Kong and Singapore are examples. Even for those benefiting from the growth of the global knowledge economy and the new technologies, economic growth and prosperity are insufficient to guarantee gender equality. Gender ideologies need to be addressed as a central element in the establishment of gender equity and equality at both state and organizational level.

Chapter 2

Researching Gender and Professional Work Cultures in Two Global Cities in Asia

This chapter backgrounds the research and considers some of the key questions that the book seeks to address on the intersection of gender, organizational change and changing work identities for women in professional labour markets. This chapter raises a number of questions that are significant in shaping the debate around gender, social, economic and organizational change. The research explores the relationship between gender, organizational change and changing work cultures in the global economy and specifically explores issues of leadership and management for women within specific organizational contexts in two global cities in Asia, Hong Kong and Singapore. In addition this chapter examines the framing of the research and also reviews a range of background literature that explores patterns of leadership and management for women in a global context, and considers the impact of global economic change and the new economy on women in professional labour markets.

Research Issues

The empirical research focuses on professional women in the context of organizational change in Hong Kong and Singapore. More specifically it explores changing work identities and patterns of leadership and management for professional women in academic and corporate life. In the process the research investigates a number of questions that are significant for women both in terms of their work identities within an organizational context and for their lives more generally. Women in a range of senior positions in academic, corporate, political and cultural life were selected as the benchmark for assessing change, not only in terms of their own lives and organizational contexts but also more broadly for the city state of Singapore and the Special Administrative Region (SAR) of Hong Kong.

A wide range of interviews was undertaken with women in senior positions in academic, corporate, political, and cultural life in both cities. The interviews conducted in Hong Kong and Singapore generated powerful, wide-ranging and important statements of women's position and, more broadly, their contribution to society. The framework for the interviews and the areas covered are outlined below.

The findings of the research are developed in Chapters 3-6 of this book. A number of significant issues emerged from the research. These include:

- Changing work identities and work cultures and the growth of the 'new economy'.
- Issues around equal opportunities and gender equity in the face of social change.
- The significance of education for women as a central factor in increasing the number of women in leadership and management.
- The importance of demographics and its impact on women and on policy debates.
- The role of foreign migrant female labour in serving the needs of advanced economies.
- Career opportunities and organizational constraints for professional women.
- Attitudes to professional women in leadership and management.
- Personal and social issues confronting professional women.
- Identification of organizational factors which promote the advancement of women into management and leadership.
- Identification of global changes which could advance the position of women in management and leadership.

The empirical research was undertaken in 2001 in Singapore and Hong Kong, while the researcher was based as a Visiting Scholar at the National University of Singapore and the Department of Sociology at the University of Hong Kong. Initial selection of women in senior academic positions had been made in advance from the websites of different universities in Hong Kong and Singapore although final selection was significantly modified on arrival in both Singapore and Hong Kong, as additional possibilities opened up. In addition, prior to going to Singapore I had been based as a Visiting Scholar at the Research Institute of the Humanities and Social Sciences at the University of Sydney. In the process of networking, a number of key individuals were identified in Hong Kong primarily, but also in Singapore, and I became familiar with their profiles prior to arrival in Asia. The objective of selection was never that of a random sample of senior women in different areas of professional life. I wanted women who had views and had something to say about the world as they saw it, critical commentators who had written about issues concerned with social and cultural change in the region, or who were involved in some capacity in formulating change in the corporate, academic, political and cultural world in the region. I wanted to interview women who had reflected on their own position, and were often professionally involved with making change happen either through the development of legislation, through holding political positions at the same time as corporate and academic positions, and who had contributed to changing the face of thinking around different aspects of life in the SAR of Hong Kong, or the city state of Singapore. The research was not about numbers, and by definition could not be, because of the paucity of women at the top. Women in top positions have only recently reached a significant mass in Hong Kong, but had not reached a critical mass in Singapore, however the impact of women as social and political commentators, as academics and as successful women in the corporate sphere could not be overlooked. Women who were solely politicians were not interviewed, as it was felt that they might reflect too closely a particular governmental line or policy focus, instead women who combined a significant involvement in politics through holding political office, at the same time as holding academic or corporate positions were interviewed, as it was felt that they reflected the sphere of professional life which I was interesting in assessing, while at the same time contributing to the debate as critically independent thinkers. Similarly women in academic and policy debates who were involved in independent think-tanks in Hong Kong and Singapore were also interviewed. In addition a number of women worked in academic and legal contexts, and also published internationally on the issues. In many cases I had read this work in advance, and had a sense of not just the contribution of these women to academic life and to the international community of scholars interested in these debates, but also to change in the region.

The selection of women in corporate life was largely made on arrival in Hong Kong and Singapore as it was easier to make direct contact by phone with these women who travelled frequently, and whose movements were more unpredictable than academic women, particularly those that ran their own companies. A number of business organizations in Hong Kong and Singapore suggested individuals, and I tried to access websites and read articles on these women before deciding if they had a perspective that might add to the debate. All the women selected were making a real contribution to their organizations in different ways and all were committed to the future success and prosperity of their countries. The women interviewed in Hong Kong highlighted the traditional international character of Hong Kong society, highlighting diversity and openness with contributors coming from China, the US, the Philippines, Britain, Australasia and Hong Kong itself. The women interviewed in Singapore were in the main Singaporeans, many educated overseas, and with diverse heritages including Chinese, Malay, Indian, but no Europeans, Americans or Australasians.

After selection was made, I sent out letters requesting interviews and including a Participant Information Sheet, Questionnaire, and Participant's Consent Form. The Questionnaire simply provided a broad framework for the interview and the interviews, which were taped, were more extensive and generally lasted around and upwards of 3 hours. All interviews were undertaken in English as neither my Mandarin (*Putonghua*) nor Cantonese exists in the real world. Some interviewees preferred to keep to the outline of the questionnaire, but were prompted to develop their thinking and ideas more fully in the process of interview, others used the questionnaire as a reference point to develop their views, their background, their work identities, their career, their involvement in different areas of social, political, corporate and academic life. In a few cases, mainly in Singapore, interviewees were not able to find time to be interviewed and simply completed the questionnaire. Unfortunately in these cases, a real engagement with the issues was not possible, and sadly in these cases the views of these women could not be fully reflected in the research, so while an occasional reference might be made to a comment on the questionnaire no fully comprehensive analysis could be given on the thinking of these women or their contribution to the academic or corporate community. The questionnaire included the following sections:

- *Career development* including sections on present position, and how the current position had been achieved, whether promotion or appointment was involved, present position in relation to position that the informant would like to achieve, present position in relation to the structure of the organization, identification of organizational or governmental policies which had assisted career development, identification of any single factor which had assisted or hampered development of career advancement. This was followed by a set of questions which asked about work conditions, including pay scales in relation to peers, hours of work, flexibility of hours of work, childcare provisions in the workplace, choice of childcare provision, provision of maternity leave, identification of any organizational barriers which hampered conditions of work.
- *Personal and social issues confronting women in leadership and management* including issues around marital status, attitudes toward being single/ being married, attitudes towards family obligations, attitudes towards accommodating husband/partner's career, support structures including maid/ servant/cleaner/nanny/housekeeper/chauffeur, spousal attitudes towards childcare and parenting, towards household and towards career.
- *Work identities and attitudes towards leadership and management* including priorities as a manager in the organization, whether women bring different qualities to the managerial role to men, and identifying what these qualities are, whether the informant defines herself as a leader in the organization, how she defines the qualities of a woman in a leadership role, how she distinguishes between a woman manager and a woman in a leadership role, whether she can identify any woman as a role model in the organization, whether she considers that women in management are expected to behave in the same way as male managers or whether women are expected to define a different style of leadership.
- *Factors advancing the position of women in leadership and management* including the question of to what extent their current organization promotes the concept of women in leadership and management, what additional organizational or other factors could assist women to move into positions of leadership and management, and what social (and global changes) have occurred to further advance the position of women in leadership and management.

All research raises problems of size or scale, while the communities of Hong Kong and Singapore are international in character, both cities can feel quite small in terms of the familiarity of their academic, corporate, political and cultural communities. Hence care needs to be taken in not only creating a high level of anonymity for those involved where it was required by contributors, and in their designations. So in many cases contributors chose to define themselves more generally in terms of a generic role within Singapore or Hong Kong rather than risk identification by any clearer institutional designation. This is understandable but did give a feeling of repetition in terms of choice of designations. I worked hard to delineate positions to avoid the feeling of flatness, particularly in Singapore. In some cases, contributors decided that part of the interview, which had no institutional reference, could be linked to them personally, and in these cases they chose to be identified. But where reference was made to any institutional context, then a very general designation was used. In the case of academics, particularly in Singapore, no disciplinary designation could be drawn on, because to identify a certain level of seniority, and to further identify subject area or institution was to identify the person themselves. For corporate women, many occupied similar positions particularly at Managing Director level, and in these cases delineation was attempted through identifying the area of work a company or a person was involved in. No identification of the current company or organization was made. In Hong Kong, some interviewees were prepared to have their identities revealed and to speak 'on the record', and some found it a useful platform, though there was absolutely no pressure to reveal identity. However in reviewing this issue and in considering the opinion of reviewers it was decided that anonymity would be retained for all interviewees. Once the interviews were completed the process of transcription was rather attenuated, as an experienced transcriber had problems with Chinese dialect, and despite having the funds from research monies to cover payment of transcriptions, I found myself spending hours writing up interviews where the transcriber had not managed to comprehend the dialect. With the transcriptions ready and checked, they were forwarded with a covering letter to the contributors, and in some cases where a consent form was still not signed this was also included. Contributors were asked to check through the transcription and to edit out or correct any errors in the transcript; most undertook this work with diligence. Designations for each individual were given in the covering letter, and informants were asked to indicate whether they agreed with the designation given or whether they wanted it changed. In some cases changes were made, and in all but one case of a contributor who was too busy completing a book on contemporary Hong Kong, transcripts were returned, corrected, and agreed. This process took one year!

One of the research issues already alluded to in work of this kind, is that with so few women in positions of seniority, individuals are readily identified and particular care was taken on this subject as indicated. Women in such positions need to feel the confidence that they can comment freely, and this will not rebound on them. This sometimes leads to reluctance to participate in such research and this did appear to be the case in Singapore more so than Hong Kong. In Singapore I received a number of refusals to participate, mainly from academic women, despite repeated attempts. Time was usually given as the reason, but women in similar positions in Hong Kong, often under considerable pressure, made the time. I began to think that more than just time was an issue here. In addition women in the most senior positions in Singapore also found the time. Where refusals occurred, I rapidly researched other 'subjects' and maintained the number of individuals to be interviewed. Corporate women seemed to regard it as more of an adventure and readily set up meetings and business lunches to undertake the interview. I did experience some of the most stunning views over Hong Kong in this way, as frequently offices were located in luxurious settings overlooking Hong Kong Harbour. One entire interview was undertaken in a restaurant and the waiters ended up drinking coffee at a side table while they waited for us to complete the interview. Academics are frequently asked to be interviewed and comment on matters and this can be advantageous in career terms, however the anonymity of such research contributions is frequently not an attractive proposition. In addition many academics are involved routinely in this kind of process as part of their own research, and thus this offers nothing new to their experience. Women in corporate life and other areas of life frequently find this process of reflection an interesting diversion, and a welcome relief from a situation that frequently affords them little in the way of such opportunities. They also seemed to find the process one where they gained in terms of personal development, almost as though undertaking a personality profile which forced them to think long and hard about issues. I received one refusal in Hong Kong from an academic, and found an immediate and very communicative replacement. The findings of the research undertaken are set out in the following chapters and makes interesting and in many cases surprising reading.

Involvement in such issues, where opinions are requested, sometimes raises anxieties around the political nature of such debates. Issues around gender and work are still a sensitive area in Singapore as can be seen by the frequent comments in the media. While political debate is opening up in Singapore, it remains a problematic matter with a lot of fear about the implications of commentary on sensitive issues. Hong Kong interestingly might be seen as going in the opposite direction to Singapore with concerns about how much open debate and commentary can be sustained in the current political climate. Whereas China has adopted a hands-off policy as regards Hong Kong up until now, many know that this may not continue. However this did not stop the informants offering significant commentary about many aspects of social change in Hong Kong and offers a rich insight into the nature of social change in Hong Kong.

Global Economic Change and Opportunity Structures for Women in Asia

In order to conceptualize the research it is important to understand the impact of economic and social change on the opportunity structures for women in Asia. Many of the countries of Asia show patterns of economic growth and socio-economic change that have transformed traditional normative structures. This is particularly evident in the shift from agriculture to industry and commerce and the accompanying urban/rural divide. While the status of women in many of these countries has improved dramatically, gender inequality is still a distinguishing feature of many Asian societies. Three countries that show such patterns are South Korea, Taiwan and Japan.

A typical example is South Korea where there are strong parallels with Japan. In both countries the shift in work cultures has not been matched by a diversification in social and cultural norms. So while women are receiving tertiary education, it is not seen as a mechanism for career advancement but for attracting higher status husbands. It is still overwhelmingly the domestic sphere that defines womanhood in Korea and women are still found predominantly in low status and low wage jobs.

The irony of this situation is noted by Hampson (2000) who observes that Korea's 'economic miracle' is in large part the result of the labour of women, working within manufacturing industries. Labour force participation for women in South Korea increased from 26.8 percent in 1960 to 47.6 percent in 1995. The expansion of the service sector in the 1990s has meant more women being employed and in 1996, 33.1 percent of women were employed in this sector (ROK, 1998, p.80). As Hampson (2000, p.176) notes: 'Women undertake the worst jobs regardless of industry ... In the clerical sector 94.7 percent of typists and 62 percent of bookkeepers are women, but only 1.4 percent of clerical supervisors are women (Chang, 1998, p.6) ... in 1995 women still earned only 61.5 percent of the average monthly male wage (ROK, 1998, p.86).'

Despite women's access to tertiary sector education, this has not been translated into opportunities in employment. Hampson notes that the labour market has been slow in accommodating women with tertiary qualifications. In 1997, only 52.5 percent of female college graduates found employment (ROK, 1998, p.66). In addition, employers are reluctant to employ women in positions of responsibility within the professions because of the social and cultural pressures encouraging women to resign on marriage. As Hampson (2000, p.180) comments: 'A professional woman's working life is expected to be very brief – less than a decade given the pressures to marry before 30 – and this makes an educated woman an expensive employee.' Social and cultural norms in South Korea work against women's position in the professions as a commitment to a career, whether in the corporate or academic sector, remains a low priority. Parental interest in educating their daughters to a high level has as its objective 'marrying up' in the social hierarchy.

The position of women in Taiwan has parallels with that of South Korea, in that while women have had constitutionally guaranteed equality with men since 1947, women's level of participation at a high level in social, economic and political life is virtually non-existent. Women's educational attainment shows a high level of achievement and figures from National Taiwan University for 1997 are as follows: women make up 48 percent of undergraduates compared to 52 percent men, 32.8 percent of masters students compared to 67.2 percent men, and 42.2 percent doctoral students compared to 57.8 percent men. Women have increasingly entered the professions traditionally dominated by men, becoming lawyers, engineers, chemists, architects, and computer scientists. Despite these improvements Chiang (2000, p.235) notes that employment rates for women have increased rather slowly since 1990. She maintains that this could be the result of women's aspirations or the inability of women to gain employment in the formal labour market. Chiang also maintains that male applicants are preferred in administrative positions requiring leadership skills, and in areas requiring professional training and technical skills, however clerical jobs and those requiring good appearance advertise for women applicants. This differentiation in type and level of appointment explains the reason why women earn sixty percent of the male wage and receive less on-the-job training and promotion opportunities. Chiang notes that: 'As a result, women are under-represented among the top level of managerial and administrative personnel (only 10 percent of top positions were held by women in 1996) while their numbers in clerical and sales sectors have grown significantly' (Chiang, 2000, p.238).

A further factor is the restrictive quota of visas for overseas workers in Taiwan, which has prevented middle-class professional women from hiring domestic help, as women do in Singapore and Hong Kong. Yi and Chang (1995) found that professional women tend to exert more influence in family decision making than women with non-professional jobs especially in the management of finance.

Despite traditional social and cultural norms that act to limit women's opportunities there is significant academic interest in the area of gender and women's rights. The University of Taiwan established the Population and Gender Studies Center. Its activities have included the organizing of seminars on issues of gender, education, health, employment, history and research methodology. The growth of a body of research literature on women in Taiwan and the availability of a wide range of Women's Studies courses at numerous universities in Taiwan has offered the potential for an emergence of new gender values, states Chiang (2000). Wang (1998) has noted that the present social welfare approach towards women's rights should be replaced by a legal rights approach.

Japan, like South Korea, shows a profile of gender equality as regards legislation and education, however despite the introduction of the Equal Employment Opportunities Law (EEOL) in 1985, gendered inequalities still abound in the workplace. In 1996, females made up only 22.9 percent of university students, social and economic factors reinforced by economic policy act against women in all spheres of work. Ambivalent attitudes towards married women entering the labour force and tax incentives discourage women from re-entering the labour force on a full-time basis after having children. Such incentives allow husbands to continue to claim their wives as dependents if they earn less than a million yen, in addition superannuating policies also discriminate against full-time working wives.

Large companies also discriminate against women, as Tipton (2000, p.216) notes: '[They] responded to the EEOL by two-track recruitment and promotion system in which a recruit chooses to apply for either the managerial or clerical track. Only the managerial track leads to top level positions in the company, but while theoretically open to both sexes, in practice male full-time employees automatically enter the managerial track whereas women enter the clerical track. Even ten years after the passage of the EEOL only 1.2 percent of women workers were at the department head level (Watabe-Dawson, 1997, p.41) and the majority of these worked for small or medium-sized companies.' Tipton also notes that other company policies also discriminate against women, such as interviewing women applicants only after all qualified male applicants have been appointed. As is typical during periods of recession, female college and university graduates found it difficult to find jobs during the 1990s in recession hit Japan.

Marriage remains an obstacle for women applying for management track positions because of the long hours and job transfers. Creighton (1996) showed that even in the department store industry, which has been one of the main industries promoting women to managerial levels, most department managers in her study have never been married. As Creighton shows: 'The corporate management practice of entertaining middle and upper-level executives in hostess clubs at night also makes it difficult for women with families to develop the networks necessary for promotion. The masculine orientation of such corporate-sponsored recreation sends the message to women that work as a full-time career is for men (Allison, 1994)' (Tipton, 2000, p.216).

Women in Leadership and Management in the Global Economy

So how have gender issues translated themselves into leadership and management positions for women in Asia and what are the implications for professional women in Hong Kong and Singapore? This section backgrounds some of the literature which explores patterns of leadership and management for women in Asia and more globally. Much of the material reflects the findings of earlier research and addresses a range of issues concerning work identities for women in senior positions in organizational life. The material considers issues such as organizational barriers confronting women, management and masculinity, issues around women and 'the glass ceiling', stereotyped attitudes to women in management, and the Asian experience. Research has shown that in all countries major barriers obstruct women's progress in management, including such obstacles as stereotypical perceptions of women's abilities and qualifications, traditional attitudes towards women's family roles, women's minimal access to the social networks from which companies recruit managers and executives, and more broadly based discrimination against women (Izraeli and Adler, 1994). Research also shows that the emergence of extraordinary women breaking through the 'glass ceiling', operating through exceptional circumstances in some countries, for example New Zealand, to assume top positions, and the mass media's heightened exposure to their presence, lead to some false assumptions about the overall success of women in leadership in these countries. Visibility had the benefit of increasing the range of role models available for women, and to breaking down stereotypical views of women's capacity to cope with leadership, but also had the impact of reinforcing the illusion that the door was now open for women to make it to the top. The article 'Breaking Glass' (*Far Eastern Economic Review*, September 26, 2003), drawing on the experience of women in leadership in New Zealand, shows that the apparent visibility of women in leadership in New Zealand does not necessarily represent the reality for professional women. Social commentator and author Anne Else claims that in the 1960s in New Zealand women won the right to challenge discrimination in appointments and women began moving into the professions in significant numbers, sometimes out-numbering men in medical and law school. On the issue of breaking the 'glass ceiling', Else sounds a cautionary note and points out that New Zealand still lags behind some European countries in the number of women in paid work and she also points out that the wage differential between men and women has actually grown. She shows that women at the top of corporations as in the position of the then Chief Executive Officer (CEO) of Telecom, is a rarity and as the Attorney General, and previously Professor of Law at Waikato University, Margaret Wilson points out, few major law firms have women partners. However Else does show there have been two women governor generals and two women prime ministers in New Zealand and thus there is something of a trend.

In Asia, the existence of large numbers of family businesses has had the impact of placing women in senior positions in corporate life. In Hong Kong where family businesses have long dominated the enterprise structure, women as well as men occupy senior management positions. In these situations, executives generally view themselves as working in the service of the family. However research shows that a woman working as an executive in a family business is not necessarily seen as qualified to assume a similar executive position in a multinational company. Studies from Hong Kong found that male managers held more prejudicial attitudes against women than female managers. The relationship between masculinity and management has been extensively researched (see Hearn, 1994, 1998, 2001; Collinson and Hearn, 1996; Hearn and Morgan, 1990) and is now frequently seen as the source of the problem as opposed to any shortcomings in women's capacity for leadership.

Research by Adler (1994, p.23) has focused on patterns of leadership and management in the transnational corporation and shows the following trends:

> Transnational corporations include women in ways that domestic, multidomestic and multinationals firms do not. First, the extremely competitive business environment forces transnational firms to select the very best people available. The opportunity cost of prejudice of rejecting women and limiting selection to men is much higher than in previous economic environments ... Second whereas domestic and multidomestic companies hire primarily local nationals, and, therefore, must closely adhere to local norms on hiring or not hiring women managers, transnational corporations are not similarly limited. Because the corporate culture of transnational firms is not coincident with the local culture of any particular country, transnationals have greater flexibility in defining selection and promotion criteria that best fit the firm's needs rather than those that most closely mimic the historical patterns of a particular country. Said simply, transnationals can and do hire local women managers even in countries in which the local companies rarely do so.

Adler also notes that US transnational companies have often hired local women managers when local firms would not. This has been particularly the case in Japan where foreign corporations have had difficulty in attracting top-ranked male applicants. Adler notes that American firms have hired well qualified Japanese women, while Japanese firms are traditionally resistant to hiring them. However, interestingly, Adler points out that Japanese multinationals operating in the US have hired more women managers in their American affiliates than they do in their home country operations. She also maintains that the greater the number of expatriates involved in the foreign affiliates, the less likely they are to restrict women managers. The company's transnational character facilitates organizational freedom and imposes a level of competitive demand not present in domestic or multidomestic environments. A further development noted by Adler as typical of patterns of appointment in the 1990s, is the trend to send women abroad as expatriate managers. As Adler interestingly notes: 'Because transnationals use expatriate and local managers, they can benefit from the greater flexibility that many cultures afford foreign women ... most countries do not hold foreign women to the same professionally limiting roles that restrict local women' (Adler, 1994, p. 23).

Antal and Izraeli (1993) in a global study of women in management, highlight the fact that with the routinization of management tasks, women remain absent from positions of authority. They also note that the size of the company does not necessarily correlate with women in positions of authority. In Italy and Japan where a large number of businesses are small and medium-sized women are concentrated in these businesses (Olivares, 1992) generally at lower level management. Multinationals have opened up the opportunities for women in management on an international basis, however there remain significant problems with the appointment of women to international assignments. An interesting assessment of the relationship between styles of management often associated with women leaders, and the representation of women in positions of leadership in one particular area of work is outlined by Harris (1998). She identifies a number of skills 'widely acknowledged as being essential for effective international managers' (Harris, 1998, p.6), which she states are those generally attributed a 'feminine style of leadership' and include 'interpersonal, intuitive and co-operative skills'. While acknowledging the importance of these skills for management roles, and in addition, acknowledging the importance of international assignments as 'prerequisites to progression to senior management positions,' Harris notes that only between 2-15 percent of managers on international assignments are women.

The globalization of the corporate world has already established the need to 'do business across national frontiers,' and Harris recognizes that the skills required are those already documented in the literature (Marshall, 1995; Rosener, 1990; Sharma, 1990) as being closely associated with a 'feminine style of management'. However as she notes, empirical research in the US and Europe (Adler, 1984; Brewster, 1991; Reynolds and Bennett, 1991) shows that the representation of women in international assignments is around 8 or 9 percent in technical expatriate positions. Some of the reasons identified for the reluctance to appoint women to international positions include 'women's lack of interest, foreigners' prejudice and organizational reluctance'. However research shows that women were not selected for international management positions despite evidence to show that 'women were as interested in international assignments as men and a lack of evidence of widespread prejudice on the part of foreigners' (Harris, 1998, p.7). There appears to be a significant discrepancy between the findings of research regarding attributes appropriate to international managers and the policy of appointments to international positions operated by multinational enterprises. The Ashridge Management Research Centre's study of 'international managers' identified the following attributes: 'strategic awareness, adaptability in new situations, sensitivity to different cultures, ability to work in international teams, language skills and understanding international marketing' (ibid., p.9). However, as Harris notes, multinational companies identify more traditional criteria in the selection of expatriate managers. The first is that expatriates are 'primarily selected on the basis of their technical competence alone' (ibid.). The second significant factor is personal recommendation from either specialist personnel staff members or line managers. 'This results in more or less predetermined selection interviews which consist more of negotiating the terms of the offer than determining the suitability of the candidate' (ibid.). Harris identifies a number of factors which make the appointment of women to international management positions problematic, they include: 'the effects of occupational segregation within the workplace; career pathing issues; and implications of the gendered nature of organizational life under which, assessments of "fit" are based on a male rather than a female profile, with negative consequences for perceptions of women's suitability and acceptability in international managerial positions' (ibid., p.10).

Adler (1994) shows that even when women are appointed to international assignments, although most of the women are sent in the same capacity as their male expatriate colleagues, some companies highlighted their hesitation by offering temporary or travel assignments rather than regular expatriate positions. Adler quotes a woman expatriate sent on this basis to Hong Kong: 'After offering me the job they hesitated: "Could a woman work with the Chinese?" So my job was defined as temporary, a one-year position to train a Chinese man to replace me. I succeeded and became permanent.' The key issue as Adler indicates is that the most salient characteristic for women expatriates on international assignments is not the fact that they are women but that they are foreign. Local managers, as Adler notes, see women expatriates as foreigners who happen to be women, not as women who happen to be foreigners. This means that the presence of foreign women in managerial positions does not necessarily improve the position for local women in management in the same companies.

Women in Hong Kong can be seen to have benefited from the traditional emphasis on familism and family businesses. De Leon and Ho (1994) indicate that professional women in Hong Kong have traditionally tended to marry later and have fewer children than other women. They also note that the proportion of managers who never marry is higher for women than for men. They maintain that the difference can be explained by the fact that more of the women managers are younger. They also highlight the fact that unlike Chinese men in Singapore, who prefer to marry 'downwards', highly educated Hong Kong men tend to marry women of similar educational backgrounds. The findings of this research confirm earlier research findings that family-centeredness persists in Hong Kong, and confirms rather than contradicts a woman's professional identity. Family influences appear to remain strong in influencing occupational decisions. Many of the women I interviewed readily acknowledge the significance of family in their career, either directly or indirectly in providing support and direction in career choice. Earlier research shows that many women entrepreneurs report that their careers have been influenced by an entrepreneurial father (De Leon and Ho, 1994, p.53) and many women business executives have fathers who were highly successful proprietors, managers or professionals. Women entrepreneurs found that kinship is not a hindrance but an asset to entrepreneurship.

Discrimination in Employment and Sex Discrimination Ordinance in Hong Kong

The transition period leading up to the handover of Hong Kong to China in 1997 was one characterized by political and legal changes. As a result of the legislation introduced during this period and the vociferous public debate about human rights, equality and equity, Petersen (1996, p.335) notes that the people of Hong Kong developed a greater awareness of human rights issues and 'women have successfully identified equality as a "human right" deserving legal protection'. A number of pieces of legislation were largely responsible for this, most noteworthy being the passing of the Bill of Rights Ordinance in 1991 and later after a hard fought battle between Anna Wu's Equal Opportunities Bill and the government's Sex Discrimination Ordinance, it was the latter that was enacted as Hong Kong's first anti-discrimination law in 1995. Such legislation, and the public debate that ensued, educated an entire population into one where expectations of success for women were the norm.

This was not the first campaign to be fought in Hong Kong on the issue of discrimination. Petersen notes that a campaign fought in the 1960s by women civil servants, led the Hong Kong government to follow a policy of equal pay and benefits for male and female civil servants. Despite this Petersen states that the government acknowledges a 'significant degree of "occupational segregation" within the civil service' (Petersen, 1996, p.347). However Petersen goes on to show that it is in the private sector: '... where sex discrimination has been most egregious in recent years. In the absence of any law prohibiting it, sex (and age) discrimination is very blatant in the Hong Kong employment market ... There is also clear evidence of pay discrimination in Hong Kong, even when women are employed in the same positions as men' (ibid.).

The Bill of Rights Ordinance was enacted in 1991. It was based on the International Covenant on Civil and Political Rights (ICCPR), including articles that prohibit discrimination, including specifically the prohibition of any discrimination on the grounds of sex. Petersen (1996, p.351) notes that the '... ICCPR also provides protection against discrimination in areas other than the specific rights recognized elsewhere in the Covenant'. Article 26 states:

All persons are equal before the law and are entitled without any discrimination to the equal protection of the law. In this respect, the law shall prohibit any discrimination and guarantee to all persons equal and effective protection against discrimination on any ground such as race, colour, sex, language, religion, political or other opinion, national or social origin, property, birth or other status.

Petersen notes that in basing the Bill of Rights Ordinance on the ICCPR, this effectively ensured its safety after handover in 1997, as Mainland China would have more difficulty in challenging the principles of the ICCPR. In June 1995, Hong Kong enacted the Sex Discrimination Ordinance, based on the provisions of the British Sex Discrimination Act. The rationale behind this legislation is outlined in Chapter 3. The Sex Discrimination Bill had one feature that appealed to women's groups in Hong Kong and to the business community and this was an Equal Opportunities Commission. As Petersen (1996, p.380) notes:

> The government's commission would not address general human rights concerns, but rather would primarily assist in conciliating complaints brought under the Sex Discrimination Bill, an approach that appealed both to the business community which hoped to avoid costly litigation, as well as to women ... The government's commission would, however, have the function of researching sex discrimination, educating the public, and promoting equality for women, thus partially fulfilling the women's movement's longstanding request for a women's commission.

However a last minute amendment was made to the legislation, limiting damages for sex discrimination to a maximum of HK$150,000. As Petersen states: 'Thus, a woman who successfully sues under the Ordinance may not recover her actual damages and may not even recover enough to pay for her legal expenses. Given the high cost of litigation in Hong Kong, this will prevent many victims from even commencing a lawsuit ...' (Petersen, 1996, p.383).

Lack of a Legislative Framework for Equal Opportunities and Equity in Singapore

Singapore's population consists mainly of immigrants and descendants of immigrants from China and India. Chan and Lee (1994) show that by 1836 only 7,229 women lived in Singapore, whereas the male population had reached 22,755. Women began to arrive in numbers in Singapore in the late 1920s and 1930s, Singapore's passage of the Aliens Ordinance in 1933, which regulated aliens' admission to the island by imposing a more expensive passage for men, facilitated this change. Large numbers of Chinese women arrived from Canton and other parts of China to work as domestic servants, others, Chan and Lee report, were kidnapped, and sold to brothels. Chan and Lee note that this generation was imbued with a strong work ethic, which they applied to the pursuit of material gain. Chan and Lee see the entry of women into the labour force in significant numbers, and particularly into management positions, as the result of the lifting of legal barriers, the growth of the economy and the availability of new opportunities in the economy for women managers. Chan and Lee note a significant turning point politically and economically for women in Singapore: 'In 1959, after Singapore became a self-governing state within the Federation of Malaysia, the governing People's Action Party (PAP) began to use the liberation of women as a prelude to liberating the country politically. The emancipation of Singaporean women was endorsed through the passage of the Women's Charter in 1961, a monogamous marriage law; the legitimization of married women's right to engage in trade and professions; the implementation from 1965 onwards of equal pay for equal work in the civil service' (Chan and Lee, 1994, p.128). Despite these developments, because post-war Singapore was burdened with a high rate of unemployment few women were employed in full-time paid jobs. The expulsion of Singapore from Malaysia in 1965 marked significant new opportunities for Singapore in terms of economic growth. 'Singapore moved quickly to develop a new strategy emphasizing the export of labour-intensive manufactured goods. The government was highly committed to creating an environment and building an infrastructure that would attract labour-intensive multinational corporate investment. The development strategy proved successful, partly due to its appropriate timing' (ibid.). As Chan and Lee note, from 1960 to 1980, Singapore experienced an annual growth rate of 9.2 percent in gross domestic product (GDP) and 13.3 percent in total trade. During this period, the demand for labour grew at an annual rate of 6 percent. Increases in women and foreign workers contributed significantly to meeting this rapidly expanding labour demand.

Women were employed at this time in three areas of work, mainly in low-income jobs, in labour intensive manufacturing, secondly in commerce and trade employing up to 19 percent of the female workforce, mostly secretaries, clerks and service personnel, and thirdly in the professional and technical sphere which accounted for 14 percent of all employed women. Most women professionals were teachers and nurses, but with increasing numbers of lawyers and doctors. Despite these increases there were still labour shortages, so Singapore adopted a selective policy of admitting foreign workers, mainly from ASEAN (Association of Southeast Asian Nations). In 1979 the government of Singapore launched a second restructuring of the economy, to move from low-wage, low-capital business activities to investment in high value- added and skill intensive activities. As Chan and Lee note, the new economic development strategy was introduced to counteract the competitive challenge of other countries in the region that were richly endowed with natural resources and cheap labour. The biggest achievement of the economic restructuring was the creation of an upgraded labour force equipped with greater skills and productivity for more value-added operations. The World Competitiveness Report 1990 ranked Singapore as the most competitive country in a group of ten newly industrialized economies. Chan and Lee note that Singaporean women benefited enormously through this process. Between 1981 and 1991 the rate of women's participation among professional and technical workers increased from 38 percent to 40 percent. During the 1980s the unemployment rate remained low at around 2 percent, in addition improvements in health care and rapid urbanization produced dramatic demographic changes in Singapore, including delayed marriage, decline in the birth rate, and extended life expectancy. The demographic pattern for the nineties remains the same with marriage being later.

To overcome the shortage in labour supply the Singapore government launched a major campaign in 1991 to attract economically inactive women back to the labour force. Despite this call, Singapore is not a signatory to the three United Nations Conventions that call for equality of the sexes in employment opportunities, in remuneration for work of equal value, and in institutional treatment in all forms. However the official governmental endorsement of women's participation in the workforce led to the growth of dual career families. As Chan and Lee note more wives now pursue their own careers, not only for personal fulfilment, but also to meet the higher expectations of lifestyle, homeownership and material comfort. So, what impact has this had on women in positions of leadership and management? The profile of women managers is not an unexpected one, most are Chinese, younger than their male counterparts and over 65 percent are married. Most have traditionally been employed in commerce, finance, insurance, real estate and business services. Many women executives are employers owning jewellery firms, boutiques, travel and employment agencies, fashion or food companies, although some are found in publishing, shipping and computer systems. Chan and Lee note that two factors have facilitated the movement of Singaporean women into management, both the result of government policies, the first the introduction of compulsory military service of 2.5 years for all men, thus delaying the movement of men into the labour force. Secondly the adoption of new university admission criteria that gave greater weight to language achievement and thus benefited women applicants, resulting in a significant increase in the number of women university students. Chan and Lee (1994, p.132) note:

> Labor statistics have consistently shown that women's labor force participation increases with education and is much higher for women who have obtained at least a secondary level education. In 1991, over 80 percent of the university educated women were in the labor force. Women workers are generally better educated than their male counterpart, with approximately 60 percent of the employed women compared to 48 percent of the employed men holding at least secondary qualifications.

Singaporean women freely say that they are the first generation of Singaporean women who benefited from greater parental awareness of the importance of education. Between 1981 and 1991 the proportion of economically active women within tertiary education more than doubled.

Despite the incredible strides women have made within Singapore as a result of changes in government policy and the expansion of the economy, there are a number of remaining barriers confronting women in Singapore. These include: the lack of a legislative framework where equal opportunities and/or equality is defined as a human right, gender stereotyping, work discrimination and inadequate networking. Gender stereotyping involves the attribution of behaviour patterns to women in senior positions, such as pettiness, inability to take risks or confront problems, and being overly calculating. Work discrimination included a preference from among newly qualified graduates, for the appointment of men, lower pay for women in terms of starting salaries, and a pattern which resulted in women taking longer to reach senior levels of management than men. Several of these patterns remain, and so concerned has the Singapore government been to address the issue of gender discrimination that a letter was published in *The Straits Times* on July 27, 2002 from the Press Secretary to the Minister for Manpower addressing the issue of gender discrimination in relation to wage rates in the civil service. The article relates the following summary made in Parliament by the Manpower Minister on the wage gap between female and male workers:

> As Manpower Minister Lee Boon Yang informed Parliament, the overall wage gap between male and female employees is due mainly to factors related to skills, qualifications, job nature, position and age not gender. One important factor is the tendency of females to withdraw from the workforce because of childcare and household responsibilities, which reduces the average years of service and working experience. Given our seniority-based wage system, this causes females as a group to earn less than males. However, a labour-market survey shows that women aged 25 to 29 actually earn more than their male counterparts with comparable skill sets, whether they work as managers, professionals and technicians, or service and sales workers. This is partly due to their early entry into the labour market (*The Straits Times*, July 27, 2002, p.29).

Apart from these more directly work related issues for women, there are also a number of more social dimensions which adversely impact on women, defined by Chan and Lee as psychological hurdles, including population policies, difficulty in locating a suitable partner, the rising number of divorces, and single parent families, and the increasing burden of physically caring for aging parents and relatives. In Singapore, as in Hong Kong, alternative arrangements to alleviate women's workload include the help of relatives, the employment of foreign domestic labour from the Philippines, Malaysia, Indonesia or even mainland China. Even with the availability of such assistance, many high-earning women feel they should still bear the primary responsibility for the care and socialization of their children. Chan and Lee (1994, p.138) also identified the high demands made on children's performance as expanding the mother's role.

> Over half of Singapore's women managers surveyed in an Asian Institute of Management study considered that the dearest price they had to pay for their career success was in the quality of relationships or time spent with the husband and children ... Some 13 percent of the women managers even felt they had missed the chance to marry because of job obligations ... the problem of involuntary single status, especially for women with higher educational attainment, may also be caused by a deeply rooted cultural value in which Singaporean men prefer to marry women who are academically and professionally their inferior. Similarly, few highly educated Singaporean women are willing to marry men of lower status then themselves ... in 1991, 76 percent of college educated women who married chose men of comparable or higher educational attainment, whereas only 55 percent of male university graduates married women of comparable educational status.

The tendency for Singapore's women managers to marry men with at least the same level of education was also reported in the Asian Institute of Management study.

Conclusion

This chapter has considered the background to the empirical research undertaken in Hong Kong and Singapore and frames the central issues and questions underlying the research. The research is contextualized in relation to the impact of globalization and organizational change on changing work identities. The specific economic, social and political contexts of social change within Hong Kong and Singapore are considered as well as gender politics within the region. More generally a range of background literature is considered which examines the position of women in leadership and management in Hong Kong and Singapore and globally, ongoing barriers confronting women in management and leadership are considered and implications for change are outlined. The framing of the findings of the empirical research are developed in the following chapters of this book.

Chapter 3

Gender Equity and Organizational Constraints in Professional Labour Markets

Central to the process of globalization and the framing of the new economy is the management of change and the emergence of new work environments. Organizational change and the restructuring of organizations has become a feature of both academic and corporate life. Whereas corporate culture has a long tradition of experiencing and managing change, for academic culture this is a relatively new experience. As has been noted elsewhere (Mackinnon and Brooks, 2001, p.5): 'In the face of increasing corporatization of universities and of the growing emphasis on technology and innovation ... the organizational cultures of universities are experiencing massive change. The direct effects of scarcer public funding restructuring and downsizing continue to reverberate through the higher education systems of Anglophone countries.' Given the recent and fragile commitment by many organizations in the 1990s to gender equity through equal opportunities policy and practice (Brooks, 1997), the question is how are these commitments faring in the new organizational environments resulting from restructuring and organizational change. This chapter examines issues around gender equity and organizational constraints in professional labour markets in the global cities of Hong Kong and Singapore.

Gendered Structures in the Labour Markets of Two Global Cities

In his analysis of global cities, Castells (1996) shows how there has been a concentration of higher level functions, power and skill in major metropolitan areas. Sassen has shown how a number of global cities including New York, London and Tokyo, predominate the global landscape. Castells goes further in identifying a number of additional cities including Chicago, Singapore, Hong Kong, Osaka, Frankfurt, Zurich, Paris, Los Angeles and San Francisco as major centres of both finance and international business. Castells further links these global cities to Asian business networks and the significant role of the state in this process. As Castells (1996, p.182) notes: 'I have empirically argued ... that at the roots of the rise of Asian Pacific economies lies the nationalist project of the developmental state. This is now generally acknowledged in the case of Japan, Korea and Singapore ... I extended the analysis to Hong Kong ... albeit with due specifications.' It has already been shown

(Chapter 2) how states in the region, driven by a nationalist agenda frequently define and determine the relationship of gender to labour markets. The following profile considers the relationship between gender equity and organizational constraints within the gendered labour markets of Hong Kong and Singapore.

Demographic profiles of global cities in Asia, particularly Hong Kong and Singapore, show a pattern of women getting married later, and having fewer children. In addition once in employment, married women are tending to have fewer children than their unemployed counterparts and married women are entering the labour force at a greater rate than unmarried women. Further, the percentage of women with secondary and tertiary education has increased dramatically. All these factors have an impact on labour markets. The question remains what patterns of gendered structuring exist in the labour markets of the global cities of Hong Kong and Singapore.

A review of the nature of gendered structuring in the labour market reveals the following patterns. The proportion of women in the financial sector in Hong Kong has dramatically increased, however key jobs in the sector remain male dominated and, in addition, the sector displays significant vertical segregation, with key managerial and professional positions being occupied by men. Women are also predominant in the professional and technical sector with this category including professions such as nursing and teaching. As Cheung (1997, p.75) notes: '... women constitute 20.2 percent of the total number of administrators and managers in Hong Kong compared with around 40 percent in the United States, 25 percent in the United Kingdom and 7.5 percent in Japan. In Singapore women occupy 18.7 percent of the legislators, administrators, and managers.' Cheung states that the significant under-representation of women at this level limits their capacity to influence governmental and other decision-making. While the income gap has narrowed for different occupational categories there remains tension in terms of the earning power of women, in societies that have always defined status in terms of money. Thus there are structural impediments towards the achievement of gender equity in the labour market.

Gendered labour markets are reinforced by a range of organizational constraints including attitudes towards women as managers and leaders. Studies that look at how women view female managers have traditionally portrayed female managers as self-reliant and goal oriented and open-minded compared with men. Studies of women's views of female managers tend to rate female managers lower on intuitiveness, sensitivity and persistence. They give lower ratings to women than to men on issues of imaginativeness, loyalty, awareness of others, and being well informed compared with men. A study of attitudes to female managers by Arnold and Lee (1990) of 700 male respondents found high ranking of such qualities as being responsible and having self-confidence as well as being intuitive and sensitive to other people. However women managers are not seen as open-minded. In relation to 'leadership ability and working style', it was women's communication skills and ability to delegate that received the highest ranking as well as having a good all-round knowledge of the business and being steady and reliable in their commitment to organizations.

However they are seen as less able to resolve conflicts and to provide motivation and to credit staff with good performance. Only 50 percent responded positively to the question of whether women could handle power and in addition it was felt that they might not be fair in their treatment of staff. Male respondents indicated a great deal of difficulty in criticizing women managers and are anxious and uneasy when receiving criticism from women managers. Of these male respondents, 80 percent worked with a female manager and over 50 percent had worked under one.

As will be shown elsewhere in this research in both Hong Kong and Singapore, men outnumber women as administrators and managers but it is noticeable that there are proportionately more female corporate managers than small business managers. This is particularly the case in Hong Kong and may reflect a different structure of opportunity in the larger more systematically managed corporations (which would include foreign-owned enterprises and MNCs) than in the smaller more patriarchal owner-managed enterprises (Westwood, Mehrian and Cheung, 1995, p.75).

Equal Opportunities and Equity

The impact of globalization and social change has been significant for both Hong Kong and Singapore. However to what extent the gender has been addressed in the process either in terms of legislation, or in terms of organizational policy and processes, has not been sufficiently researched. Some of the issues emerging from this research highlight the fact that even when policy is in place organizations frequently fail to implement policy in an adequate way. Hong Kong in legislative terms is considerably more advanced than Singapore in its commitment to anti-discrimination policy and to institutional equality, if not in its informal structures.

Hong Kong implemented the Bill of Rights in 1991, prior to handover to China in 1997. A Senior Lecturer in Law at the University of Hong Kong notes that: 'For women it was a real door of opportunity because there were equality provisions in the Bill of Rights. They did, I think, a very good job of identifying equality as a human right. They did an excellent job of making people understand that human rights wasn't just free speech, freedom of association, freedom of movement, that it included a right of basic equality.' The passing of the Bill of Rights Ordinance in 1991 paved the way for the Equal Opportunities Ordinance, under the guidance of Anna Wu who was also a member of the Legislative Council in Hong Kong. However the government introduced a competing bill in 1994, which was more limited in scope, the Sex Discrimination Bill, which included a dimension proposed by Anna Wu, but rejected by the Executive Council, this was the Equal Opportunities Commission. The pressure on the government to introduce these major pieces of legislation was no doubt in part the result of the work of significant women opinion leaders in Hong Kong, including Anna Wu and Christine Loh. So, in reality, what has been the impact of these pieces of anti-discrimination legislation? (See Petersen. 2002, 2000, 1999.) Such legislation facilitates the development of institutional equal opportunities policy.

Organizational Policy and Practice

If we take the University of Hong Kong as an example of where equal opportunities
policy and practice can be assessed in organizational terms, the University of Hong
Kong has an explicit equal opportunities policy but not an affirmative action policy.
A Dean at the University of Hong Kong indicated that the University had the first
full-time equal opportunities officer, but commented that: '...unfortunately he's a
man.' I asked her about the impact of an equal opportunities policy and an equal
opportunities officer on women at the University of Hong Kong, and she responded
as follows:

> I think currently in the university, there isn't any obvious disadvantage to being a woman.
> I think we are provided with an environment which is supportive to people. Performance
> is based on objective standards. For example, previously in the Department of ... all
> our senior lecturers and chair professors were men, now we have three women who are
> readers/professors. In the wider university, there are women professors in Medicine,
> Social Work and Education, another one in the English Department, who is Chinese, from
> the US. You can basically count them on two hands.

A less generous view was held by a Professor at the University of Hong Kong:

> ... there is no VC [Vice-Chancellor] in Hong Kong, nor has there ever been, whatever
> they chose to call themselves, and some like to be called president, most prefer 'god', who
> have ever supported equality policy within the university. We couldn't even get them to
> write job advertisements in a non-sexist way. There is an Equal Opportunities Committee
> that was set up in the university. But there is no understanding at a senior level, meaning
> Pro Vice-Chancellor and chair professor or Vice-Chancellor of what equal opportunity
> employment policies are.

She cited cases of sexual harassment at the University of Hong Kong in terms of the
university's failure to really understand the nature of equal opportunities policy. As
she noted: '... the response of the university has been utterly inappropriate. They just
haven't known what to do ... both these cases [of sexual harassment] went to court,
they involved criminal activity, and the university brushed them off as boys high
jinks, and didn't want to take any tangible action for fear of damaging the long term
future of high spirited boys, who must be boys.'

Anti-discrimination legislation, of course, also covers issues of racial
discrimination. A Senior Programme Director in Hong Kong believed that racist
attitudes, even overt racism, were certainly prevalent in Hong Kong, in fact she had
had an immediate experience of such attitudes. 'I was at a dinner party, with the former
Vice-Chancellor [of the University of Hong Kong, since resigned] ... he said, at that
dinner party, I won't be truly happy until I see the last *kweiloh* (white devil) leave
this institution. So, you know, I wasn't the only *kweiloh* at the table. I was certainly
the only woman.' The issue of racism in Hong Kong was an issue also discussed
with a professor at the University of Hong Kong, who identified being white and not
speaking Chinese as factors that had hampered her career. She made the point that

she was not making a strong case for any serious hampering of her career and said that people needed to remember that they are in a Chinese society. As she indicated: '... I mean do they think that being white somehow gives them an edge. For most of Hong Kong's history, the power and the racism was the other way. So if the tables are now turned, none of us has to be here. Virtually everybody has somewhere else to go.' I asked her whether she thought racism exists within university culture in Hong Kong. She responded with reference to the University of Hong Kong as follows: 'If you mean institutionalized racism, no. If you mean informal racism, yes. And I have no doubt that the previous Vice-Chancellor was racist ... but there is a very strong feeling amongst local people that having tolerated a hundred and sixty odd years of British domination, its now their turn.' A Chair Professor in Medicine in Hong Kong, commenting on issues of equal opportunities and equity, felt that a meritocracy best described the situation in Hong Kong. She maintained that there is a tendency now to be more politically correct in appointments but she did not think it was fair to say that meritocracy had taken a backseat. She did not think things had significantly changed since colonial days, if you are good then you get the opportunity.

In Singapore, equal opportunities policy is not something that has been addressed by either government or institutions in any legalistic sense. In 1979 the United Nations (UN) General Assembly ratified the Convention on the Elimination of All Forms of Discrimination Against Women (CEDAW). This document was then submitted to national governments for ratification by their respective legislatures. Singapore is not a signatory to this convention and has made no commitment to equal opportunities or equity in its policies.

Chan (2000) characterizes Singapore as a patriarchal authoritarian state and maintains that the policies of the People's Action Party's (PAP), which is the party of government, are accepted and tolerated because it has successfully provided for the economic and social needs of the population. Women have benefited in a number of areas including education, employment and health, however the overriding patriarchalism of the government is reflected in a range of policies. Women in Singapore do not have the right to equal pay for equal work, as Singapore did not sign the UN convention which included: equal pay for equal work for men and women; eliminating discrimination against women; and equal opportunities and treatment for men and women.

There are a number of areas where discrimination is apparent. The labour force participation rate (LFPR) for married women in Singapore is much lower than that for married men. In 1997, the LFPR for married women was 48 percent while that for married men was 86 percent. For single women it is almost equal that of single men, 66 percent compared to 67 percent (Singapore Department of Statistics, 1998, p.6). In addition in the 1990s men's income grew faster than women's income. The average monthly wage for men grew by 13 percent while that for women rose by only 8.3 percent. Chan (2000, p.43) argues that this is due to the widening of the income gap between men and women due to faster occupational upgrading among males. Overall, 26 percent of men in Singapore and 11 percent of women work in highly paid occupations (Yim and Ang, 1997).

The Women's Charter was passed in Singapore in 1961, however it is primarily concerned with the roles, responsibilities, duties and rights of women within the family. Chan notes that the Singapore government's policies have shown progressively that while women's rights in the family should be protected by law, it is men who are and should be treated as head of the household. As Chan (2000, p.48) observes: '… state-endorsed patriarchy means that both men and women are allocated separate duties and responsibilities.'

Most of the women interviewed in Singapore did not raise the issue of equal opportunities. In addition the application of a gender analysis to policy at any level in Singapore is not a very well developed one. An Associate Professor at a university in Singapore was the only woman interviewed in Singapore who identified the gender issue as an organizational barrier. An Academic Administrator at the National University of Singapore discussed the issue of the 'glass ceiling' in different disciplinary areas and pointed out that in the Faculty of Medicine at the university there is a quota on the supply of females. She explained the reasoning behind the quota: 'This is due to economic reasons, because they think that … to admit a female, [they] would have to invest \$200,000 in her, and after becoming a doctor she goes off and takes maternity leave, then my investment is not as worthwhile as if I had invested in a male. But this is due to the kind of economic reasons.' The lack of equity in this situation along with the fact that women civil servants are not allowed the same medical benefits as their male colleagues is now the subject of debate in parliament, in the media and within the public.

Career Opportunities and Organizational Constraints

There has long been a concern that women play a very small part in the higher levels of university management (Mackinnon and Brooks, 2001, p.6). The issue of corporate restructuring within organizations generally, and more specifically within universities, raises significant issues for gendered patterns of management. There are differing views as to the impact of the current organizational change within universities and higher educational institutions generally.

> Some are optimistic that the new climate offers potential for change. Yeatman, for instance, sees possibilities for those 'literate in the new technologies of governmental management' to capitalize on its supposed transparency and accountability and to open up 'the policy process of universities to issues of equity and participation' (Yeatman, 1995, p.104). Others are not so optimistic (Currie, 1995; Payne, 1998).

What becomes clear from the findings of the research is that while there are differences between the cultural context of organizational life in Hong Kong and Singapore which afforded different opportunities and different experiences for women in senior positions in organizational life, many of the issues confronting academic women in Hong Kong and Singapore are the same as, and accord with, the experiences of academic women (and some academic men) in countries such as the UK, Australia and New Zealand (see Brooks and Mackinnon, 2001). There are even stronger parallels between corporate life in Hong Kong and Singapore at the very top for women, although women in the upper echelons in corporate life in Singapore have not reached a critical mass. As already noted, in many Chinese diasporic communities in the corporate world, there are also close links between business and family, particularly in Hong Kong, outside the context of multinational organizations. It is in these organizations where some women are reaching the upper levels of management although a direct comparison with MNCs at least in terms of specifically designated positions, is difficult to assess. There are some interesting differences superficially between women in corporate and academic life, and as I have noted elsewhere (Brooks, 2001), the organizational context of academic life affords successful women fewer opportunities to get to the top. Corporate life appears to be more prepared to change more rapidly, to appoint and recognize women's contribution, and affords women more responsibility, and decision making opportunities than academic life. Academic women, at least from the findings of this research, are often very happy with the intrinsic satisfaction afforded by the work, and on a personal level are, for often very sound reasons, not seeking positions at the top of academia. As many senior women interviewed commented, they wanted to balance quality of life with life at the top, this speaks volumes about the changing nature and corporate restructuring of academic life (Brooks and Mackinnon, 2001) which makes it both a harsh and unrewarding organizational context for successful academic women. The issue of balancing quality of life with career demands is explored in Chapter 5.

The restructuring of academic life has been accompanied by a new corporate managerialist ethos, and the translation of hitherto academic positions into management positions. In Hong Kong and Singapore, universities have only recently appointed women into senior management positions. The position of Dean is a case in point, with the two foremost universities in Hong Kong and Singapore, the University of Hong Kong and the National University of Singapore, showing similar patterns in this regard. It is also interesting that women should appear for the first time in these positions at a time when universities are going through a process of corporate restructuring and women put in these positions are often in the frontline in relation to both staff hostility and university executive pressures. A Dean at the University of Hong Kong outlined some of the difficulties: 'The Dean of a university is an elected position. It is a half time position compensatory to the department. So it isn't a very prestigious position, I haven't got a lot of responsibility nor authority. So nobody really likes to do things like this, at a time when there are enormous pressures for publication, academic achievements and all that.' This Dean saw herself as an agent of change, she said: 'You could describe me as an entrepreneur', she had revamped the entire curriculum on an interdisciplinary basis to accord with the university's desire to restructure along Faculty rather than departmental lines.

Some of the same issues had been encountered by a Senior Academic Administrator in Singapore, who had experienced resistance to change from a range of different groups, particularly from the grass roots academics. She expressed the inherent conflict for academic women of accepting senior administrative positions when their primary emphasis and focus is scholarship. It is in fact a conflict for many academics in terms of academic achievement and a position to reflect that, and the demands and responsibilities inherent in the position of academic administrator. She expressed the dilemma in the following way: '... my immediate thought reviews the bifurcation in my mind, because I was thinking well I'd really like to be a professor, so the academic side of me said something, and then the administrator side said, well I think I've got my hands full.' When the point was made that the two are not exclusive and that promotion to professorial level can come through administrative responsibilities, her response was as follows:

> Well, I think as an institution that's something we still have to work out. We have established, in principle, that one could become professor if you're good at teaching, and in contribution to administration, but there must be a minimum threshold one has met in the academic world. At the risk of sounding self-congratulatory, I think I have reached that threshold academically. But I think for my own self, I would not really want to see myself as a professor based on my administrative work. I see myself as being a professor on the basis of my academic work

A Reader/Professor at the University of Hong Kong had taken action to alleviate the administrative burden and to create space for research and writing. She had chosen to move to a fractional appointment for three years which means she had dropped to 60 percent salary and benefits:

> I was bogged down in administrative detail, which bores me stupid, I've done so much of it, it's just no longer a pleasure. And in a university environment which is increasingly harsh in terms of funding. The job of head [of department] for instance I think is an appalling job. It's about managing much less, and having to produce a great deal more with it.

Entrepreneurial Focus

Being a risk-taker or an entrepreneur is something that tends to have been associated with corporate culture, and is frequently related to the organizational context in which individuals find themselves. Being a risk-taker or having an 'entrepreneurial' focus was something that characterized many of the senior women in both corporate and academic life in this research. This was a particular feature of the women interviewed in Hong Kong, who had frequently shifted countries to take up different positions or been prepared to take on additional skills and qualifications mid-career to enhance their career potential. Both the Senior Educational Administrator within the legal profession in Hong Kong and the Senior Programme Director at the University of Hong Kong had undertaken advanced academic qualifications on a part time basis with overseas universities in the time they had been in Hong Kong, and the latter had also undertaken part-time unpaid work for a professional legal grouping in Hong Kong to offset her frustrations with her current position. Several women had also taken on significant areas of additional responsibility either through holding political positions as in the case of a political- opinion leader in Hong Kong, or through her work in the field of Hong Kong legislation, as in the case of a Senior Lecturer in Law at the University of Hong Kong, or through their work with community groups, as in the case of a Dean at the University of Hong Kong.

In some cases the level of commitment to serving in both political positions alongside either corporate or academic positions seemed to take on the profile of a 'dual career' as in the case of the Chair-Professor in Medicine in Hong Kong, as well as in the case of the political-opinion leader in Hong Kong. While several academic women described themselves as 'entrepreneurs', two corporate women had quite clearly defined entrepreneurial profiles. A Senior Vice-President of a company in Singapore, and one of a small group of women holding a seat on the Board of a company in Singapore, had climbed the corporate ladder and had had her contribution recognized and at 40 was clearly a corporate success story, confident, and with a very supportive company behind her. She started with the company as a sales person and over the years had climbed the corporate ladder to be a manager and eventually to a director level, and then up to the current level of Senior Vice-President. Her portfolio had widened from marketing and sales to include functions like R&D (Research and Development), manufacturing, purchasing, and so on. When I initially talked to a Managing Director of an aviation company in Hong Kong, we discussed how she had moved at the request of her brother from Estee Lauder in Hong Kong, as he had wanted someone who he could rely on personally. Business aviation, she advised me, requires a very personalized kind of networking and requires moving in the right circles. She was initially skeptical about the idea and particularly with the 'handover' to China in 1997, she felt that this would have a big economic impact on the region, and that the market for traveling in private corporate jets would not be a big one. In addition she also had some personal issues with the move. She said it was unusual for a woman to be in this area of work, probably globally, but certainly in Asia. I asked her whether she ever worried about being isolated as a woman in a male dominated industry. She said she did not worry about this and has relied on her networking skills and adventurous marketing strategy to succeed. She has also acted in a facilitating and educating mode as many of the companies in China sought consultancy services. She saw herself as an entrepreneur, always prepared to take risks, and had always had that spirit even before joining the aviation company.

Gender Politics as a Career Issue

The issue of gender politics as an aspect of organizational structures has been well documented in the literature. Issues of age and gender frequently intersect in these politics in the Asian context, given the patriarchal character of Chinese communities and organizational structures (Chan, 2000). A Senior Academic Administrator in Singapore was told that it was her age, rather than her gender, that would potentially be a source of difficulty for her colleagues to accept; she was 36 at the time of the interview. In discussing the issue of age as an organizational constraint in terms of career opportunity, this academic woman went on to identify age as the single factor that hampered her career development. She said that she felt a preference for older people was an Asian thing. I asked her whether she considered this to be something both male and Asian. She responded as follows: '… in my particular case as much about age as gender … I had a very senior colleague, about 60 years old, male of course, say to other people, I will never work under a 36 year old female – the emphasis seemed to be as much on age as it was about gender.' In some cases it is the cultural as much as the organizational context that frames gender politics. I asked a Senior Educational Administrator for legal education in Hong Kong whether she had any views of being a woman, and an expatriate woman, in the Hong Kong legal system and whether this had posed any obstacles for her in her profession. She thought that the Hong Kong Bar Association was not the problem. The problem that an expatriate female barrister meets in Hong Kong is with solicitors and secondary clients, particularly in criminal work. 'Criminal clients do not like females, and they particularly do not like expatriate females. So your work there is very limited. And solicitors, apart from matrimonial matters, are not keen on instructing expatriate women. I'm not sure about Chinese women.'

The very corporate world of commodities trading in Hong Kong is an area where one might expect to find some prime examples of gender politics operating. A very well-known political-opinion leader in Hong Kong is CEO (Chief Executive Officer) and founder of Civic Exchange in Hong Kong, an independent policy think-tank. A former politician, member of the Legislative Council (LegCo), and senior executive in corporate life, she described her experience of the world of commodities trading as a very male dominated business, by and large done by men. 'They hung around in packs and there were different packs. I really didn't fit into any of these packs. For example the pack leaders would go out for drinks, or they would go into each other's offices and the elders would hold court with younger traders, and they would have their beers and their whiskies.' She drew on her 'people skills' to carve out an independent managerial role for herself. In addition her ability to communicate cross-culturally proved a huge advantage in a multinational company.

> I found that because of my background and being able to understand my colleagues, from their perspective, (people from Asia, people from Hong Kong), I was able to actually talk to people overseas more effectively as a 'cultural bridge'. And because I was a cultural bridge, I found that over the years people started to rely on me, or to ask me to be the 'cultural translator', of what was really going on.

Another aspect of gender politics in the context of work identities is the level of community activism undertaken by a number of the women interviewed. Women professionals at all levels tend to involve themselves more in the activities of the community. The nature of change in Hong Kong particularly around the areas of human rights and anti-discrimination policy, as well as the social impact of the 'hand-over' in 1997 has led to a wide range of social as well as political problems emerging. Many women interviewed played a significant part in the Hong Kong community; their work identities were frequently tied in with their commitments outside the organization.

A Senior Lecturer in Law at the University of Hong Kong is a person whose contribution to the academic community and to different aspects of the law in Hong Kong gives her a stature and reputation that extends well beyond her academic position. She had, since her arrival in Hong Kong in 1989, with a Harvard Law School background and experience of corporate litigation in the US, always been actively involved with Hong Kong jurisprudence. Her involvement in the development of such legislation as the Bill of Rights Ordinance, and anti-discrimination legislation in Hong Kong in conjunction with Anna Wu, had only emerged when she arrived in Hong Kong. She said it was because she took equality for granted in the US. She indicated that if she had stayed in the US and had hit the 'glass-ceiling', she may well have felt differently and she also said that on issues generally she would take a pro-feminist stance. In Hong Kong she found it upsetting to see so much discrimination, and also to see that it was so blatant and so accepted: 'People didn't feel the least bit embarrassed about saying, only a man can do that job. People didn't seem the least bit embarrassed about the fact that women in certain villages in the New Territories couldn't vote in village elections. They just accepted that as normal and that really upset me.' She had combined her academic scholarship with her involvement with local issues of academic freedom, anti-discrimination legislation and jurisprudence and had published both in Hong Kong and internationally on these issues. A Dean at the University of Hong Kong had also extended her expertise to areas of work in the community, particularly with divorced women, children whose parents are in prison, and had developed a model of grief and bereavement counseling in Hong Kong. She had also worked with a group of people to promote social work education in China and was proud of these achievements. She saw her market as a local one and had published extensively locally. She was also an advocate within the university for student participation, and also actively promoted academic (and other) women's interests. It is clear that effecting change within their organizational context, and indeed a social context within the community, was something that was central to their work identities.

Promotion and Organizational Constraints

Promotion is something that has organizational dimensions, but can also be about individual identities and personal aspirations. The point has been made elsewhere that academic organizations appear slower to change and reward successful women than corporate and other institutions (Brooks, 2001). Organizations adopt a range of strategies to address the issue of promotion from financial rewards, to 're-titling', to a significant emphasis on transparency of procedure. The findings of this research show a full range of organizational constraints and individual aspirations and grievances.

Uniformity within academic institutions on a global basis as regards any criteria including promotion has long disappeared. Many universities have gone through radical corporate restructuring processes (Brooks and Mackinnon, 2001) and certainly there are great difficulties for academics to make any sort of comparison between countries. The University of Hong Kong has developed a hybrid model, which for many has alleviated the promotion issue and as the pay for academics is exceptionally generous by global standards, academics find themselves carrying titles and remuneration packages, which those in other countries may have taken a entire career to achieve. The hybrid model attempts to accommodate the British and American models. Within the British system the position of 'professor' is the equivalent of 'reader', but readers are not called professors. However to accommodate the American system, readers at the University of Hong Kong are called 'professors'. So these positions are not the equivalent of a chair-professor, which is a considerable jump from reader, which requires a formal promotion. This is also the case with the move from senior lecturer to reader, unlike the Australasian system which requires a move from senior lecturer to associate professor, to full professor. The University of Hong Kong underwent a 're-titling exercise' in 1996 and academics could choose if they were already in the position and wanted to keep the title. People who were appointed after the change in titles had to accept the new titles. Despite this attempt by the University of Hong Kong to address concerns about promotion issues, there are still concerns around promotion and publications for academics. A Dean at the University of Hong Kong who held a reader/professor position, was not interested in applying through the formal promotion channels for a chair-professor position, because her publications are local, written in Chinese and intentionally so, because she writes for a local market. So she recognizes that under the current academic system, chances of promotion would be slim. 'I have written almost ten books, hundreds of articles, and I see writing as a form of advocacy. So now I've reached this point I'm fairly satisfied to go on until retirement. Being a chair professor, I would have to write reports to the vice-chancellor every year, and the dean would assess performance in all of these, so I would have less freedom.' In Singapore, an Assistant Professor (promoted subsequent to the interview to Associate Professor) had tried for promotion for over 5 years, and had been refused and speculated that it was to do with her political activism. As she noted: '... this would just be assumption on my part, but I assume that part of the reason that my promotion did not come as fast as it should have, had to do with my insistence on taking certain political positions, and my willingness to do that. That is something I am proud of.'

Despite the 're-titling exercise' at the University of Hong Kong, certain academic areas were not covered by this process. A Senior Programme Director in the area of continuing education had been in the same position as she had been for the last ten years, as there had been no promotion exercise during that time. The type of work undertaken by this unit frames it as an extension of the university, dealing with professional training and thus primarily focused on teaching rather than research. Since this unit is primarily concerned with generating new courses and large numbers of students, staff carry very heavy teaching loads and carry titles that acknowledge their course related role. Thus regardless of carrying a large amount of responsibility, this Senior Programme Director had been sitting at the top of the assistant professor scale for 8 years. Subsequent to the interview, I was advised that this Senior Programme Director has now taken over and leads the unit. However an update on her position in this role revealed continuing frustrations and a lack of transparency in its operation. She describes the situation:

> The Headship, it transpires, is virtually a farce. All responsibility, no autonomy. No budgetary control, no staffing control, and little opportunity to be 'strategic'. The Directorate maintains a 'power over' mentality, indicating on more than one occasion recently that delegation and autonomy to heads will occur once sufficient managerial 'maturity' is demonstrated by us. Meanwhile there certainly has been no attempt to groom any of us to reach the 'appropriate' level of maturity whatever that might be.

In some cases there was a clear lack of interest in promotion issues. A Senior Research Fellow at a research unit in Singapore said that the organizational structure was quite flat, and researchers operated with a high degree of individual autonomy. She had joined the unit as a Research Fellow and had moved up to Senior Research Fellow. She said of her current position: 'I am pretty happy with where I am right now ... I came in knowing what the structure is like. That this is a very flat organization. So ... I get satisfaction out of doing the kind of work that I do, rather than, you know, in terms of promotional prospects, especially in terms of position.' A Research Fellow based in Singapore held a similar view; in fact promotion had never really crossed her mind or bothered her. Again in terms of remuneration, such jobs are well paid and are equivalent to a university position and well above the average salary range for equivalent positions in the UK and Australasia. I asked the Research Fellow about issue such as recognition for her work and her response was as follows:

> Well, you know, you get pats on the back now and then. Really, it sounds rather strange but I'm doing it out of interest. I could drop out anytime. I don't feel that I really need the job, but the job gives me the mental space, the time, pays me for it, to forward my research interests ... I have a baby at home and he would love for me to be there all day. So I know it sounds kind of strange, but it's not really a career as such.

A Senior Lecturer in Law at the University of Hong Kong held similar views regarding promotion. I asked her whether she felt that the lack of promotional opportunities could be offset by remuneration and whether she worried about her career in this regard. She responded as follows:

> Not really. This may be personal to me, but if I never get promoted, it won't bother me particularly much. I like my job, actually I love my job. I love what I do. I don't feel underpaid, and I don't worry as much as some people about the lack of promotion. I do feel that we're not getting the recognition we deserve. I sympathize with that view. It's just not one that particularly affects me.

The number of academic women who had reached the top in both Hong Kong and Singapore were very few indeed. However a Chair-Professor in Medicine in Hong Kong had found the promotion process and indeed the path to the top in academic and political life seemingly very smooth. I asked her, given the fact that there were so few women in such senior positions in Hong Kong universities, whether there was anything she could identify in terms of her career that led to her considerable achievements. She said that some of the reasons she had reached the top of her profession were a combination of factors including being very focused, the fact that she chose an area where there was not too much competition, and which not too many doctors wanted to specialize in. She felt that her research and its significance led onto government appointments, culminating in being asked to join the Cabinet of the last Governor of Hong Kong (Chris Patten), before that she had been appointed to the Legislative Council in Hong Kong.

The corporate sector appeared to offer considerably more potential for promotion and, at least on the surface, greater recognition for those involved. A Senior Vice-President of a company in Singapore said that she joined the company when it was a relatively young company and worked with the founder and the core team to build the company. She said that as the company has grown, her contribution has been recognized, and she has been given promotion. One of the factors that she identified as beneficial was the company's policy of promotion from within.

> We strongly encourage that, and believe that internal people have every potential or the capability to be groomed, that would be our first priority. The company also has a training and development programme for staff, to get them ready to handle more responsibilities. Also I think this is a company which I find has very little politicking. So productivity is really more important than how to get a promotion … So we really go by the true substance of the individual.

Perhaps not unexpectedly few senior women in corporate and academic life could identify factors that assisted their career development compared to those who identified factors that hampered their career development. An Assistant Director at the National University of Singapore (NUS) outlined an organizational factor that benefited Singaporean academics at NUS. She explained that at NUS there are expatriate faculty members who applied for their positions and there are also Singaporeans who graduated from the university and: '… we are kind of groomed to come back and teach. So we are offered scholarships, I had a scholarship at Masters level, and I had a scholarship for my PhD, to do my PhD in the US.' She went onto explain that this group of individuals are appointed as Senior Tutors before they go abroad, and when they return they are appointed as Assistant Professors at NUS. I asked whether this meant that the returned scholars are more likely to go in the direction of promotion into top positions than academics coming in from elsewhere. Her response was as follows: 'More likely to assume responsibility I would say compared to people who come from the outside. Partly also because this is a national university, so they try as much as possible to have local people in the administration.

But of course in some cases they would also invite the non-Singaporeans when they prove they are good.' (This scheme has now been withdrawn from NUS.)

A wide range of factors was identified by professional women as hampering career development. These included:

- Children and family.
- Visibility/time in the office (in Singapore).
- 'Culture of fear' (in Singapore).
- 'Lousy bosses' (in Singapore).
- Not speaking Chinese (in Hong Kong).
- Being expatriate and white (in Hong Kong).
- Competency of support staff (in Hong Kong).
- Individual failings.

As might be expected, the largest number of women identified children and family as the main factor that hampered their career, even above those factors of organizational constraints. The following response from a Senior Programme Director in Hong Kong sums up the feeling:

> I am afraid family as opposed to this institution. I have actively decided to support my husband's career, which has meant not taking risks in mine, and because of the nature of his career, I have been the primary caregiver to our two children. So, I mean it's a very uncomfortable thing to think even, and say, but outside my organizational context, if I were to say one major factor that has held me back, then my decision to invest time and energy in my family ... I'm pretty sure I would have taken more risks had (name of husband) been in a more stable situation.

Another related factor, identified by several women, was being in the 'sandwich generation' and having responsibility for both children and elderly parents. The implications of this were identified by a Deputy Head of Department at a university in Singapore, in terms of time and the ability to stay late in the office. As this academic woman pointed out she would not want to stay in the office until 9 pm but prefers to spend time with her children and family. The issue of visibility in the office is an interesting one, and appears to be a factor for academic and corporate women in both Singapore and Hong Kong. While office time is essential for any occupation, the flexibility provided by the new technology does not seem to be something that has really become part of organizational culture for senior figures in any mainstream way. It appears from the findings of this research that the flexibility to work at home using the new technology is really only partly accepted by both academic and corporate life. Despite this, many academic women did express the fact that they had flexibility in their workplace up to a point.

An Associate Professor at a university in Singapore described the 'culture of fear' that she felt had hampered her career. This was to do with the need to control what individuals say, and she felt that this is still a pervasive problem in Singapore. She defined herself as being an independent thinker and therefore difficult for organizations because of the problem of attempting to control her comments when it was never entirely clear what she would say. A Deputy Director of a research unit in Singapore described 'lousy bosses' as the main factor that had hampered her career, although she was not specific in terms of how they were unsatisfactory. This does seem to be a common preoccupation in Singapore to blame bosses and may have something to do with supposed remoteness of local managers from their employees.

Both academic and corporate women in Hong Kong identified not speaking Chinese as a factor which hampered their career, but the expatriate women recognized that it was their choice to stay in Hong Kong and not to learn Chinese, these included a Senior Educational Administrator, a Professor at the University of Hong Kong, and a Senior Lecturer in Law at the University of Hong Kong. The first two combined the issue of not speaking Chinese with the added barrier of being expatriate, or being white. A Senior Educational Administrator for the legal profession in Hong Kong combined being expatriate with being 'mature' and female as a particular problem with barristers in Hong Kong. The issue of 'racism' within an organizational context in Hong Kong is an issue identified by a number of individuals and has already been dealt with. A Managing Director in Hong Kong combined what she regarded as an individual failing with the issue of not being able to communicate effectively in Chinese: 'My impatience, and sometimes I tend to make rash decisions, and I'm also a very direct speaking person … that has cost me major pains in the past, business-deal-wise.' She also regretted that, while she could speak Chinese, she could not write Chinese because she was educated at an English language school. She felt that this hampered her ability to do business in China, as she had to rely on her managers in mainland China to communicate. Another corporate woman in Singapore identified the lack of competency in support staff as a factor hampering her career: 'It's more an issue of competency … I feel that in Singapore we have grown so fast that people may not have reached a certain level, but have been promoted because of opportunities. So some people, while they are called managers, they lack the actual experience.'

Career Aspirations

There appeared to be a distinct difference in the aspirations of corporate and academic women in relation to the position they indicated they would like to achieve in the organization. As outlined earlier, academic life no longer holds the appeal for academic women that it once did, and the findings of this research indicate that many are now looking to quality of life over and above that of success at the top. The following comments from a Professor at the University of Hong Kong, while they may be seen as applying to the situation in one university, can equally be seen to apply to academia more generally:

Once upon a time, if you had asked me that question, say seven years ago, I would have said without doubt, that I wanted to be chair/professor. If not here, then somewhere. The somewhere probably would have been Australia rather than the UK. But, I think the environment of the university has changed very markedly in those seven years. The focus on, as they see it, whoever they are, cutting fat. The decision to employ all new staff on contract, rather than offer tenure, and the decision to make those contracts three years rather than five, I think has fundamentally altered the environment, the intellectual environment of the university. So inputs, outputs, emphasis on raising research grants as an input measure related to output ... it became obvious to me after a while, that what I had wanted, was no longer what I wanted ... The chair professor's job is okay, but in order to have any chance of that I would have had to have been head of department. I refused three times to be head of department, which I did knowing it would almost certainly mean there would be no more career advancement for me. But the job is so unpleasant these days that I really felt that I didn't want to do it.

Several academic women found that they gained greatest fulfilment from the intrinsic satisfaction of their work, be it teaching or researching and that a senior managerial position either held no appeal for them or posed significant dilemmas. A Senior Programme Director said her interest was very much anchored in student centred issues and she gained a lot of her self-esteem and 'buzz' from the classroom. So she felt that moving further into managerial issues and away from her 'grassroots', could make her less happy, and posed a dilemma. A Senior Lecturer in Law at the University of Hong Kong also found her greatest satisfaction in being an academic rather than being a manager:

I might be different from some of the women that you've interviewed, but I really don't have any aspirations to be head of department, or dean or associate dean. I have the feeling that somewhere along the way, as I get older, I will be asked to do some of these things ... and if so I will do it. But it's not something I am jumping up and down wanting to do. The advances that I want to make are in my own research, not within the organization particularly. I'm happy with my position in the organization, really I am.

I asked her whether she had aspirations to academic leadership in the organization, for example as a chair professor as opposed to a head of department. Her response reflected comments made by other successful academic women about organizational constraints they confronted at the University of Hong Kong, in particular the problem of promotion, and the nature of the organization:

If I could take on a leadership role in things like encouraging research and teaching development and curriculum reform ... I'd be happy to do that. But things like chair-professor at Hong Kong University are just completely on the other side of the planet. I mean you can't even get a Senior Lecturer very easily, so the idea of a chair professor would be pretty much beyond the pale. So I don't even think in those terms.

By contrast corporate women defined their work identities more closely with the position of the organization and the organization's success. In these cases individual success was closely allied to that of corporate success. A Senior Vice-President of a company in Singapore felt that while she was quite satisfied with her current position, there was much she could do to take the company to the next level of success: 'As for the future what do I see, I think my greatest hope is to grow this business to eventually become, perhaps an independent company by itself. Instead of just a business unit, it could become an independent legal entity.' When I indicated that she seemed quite relaxed and confident about future prospects, she responded as follows: 'I think the fact that I have many years of working experience, especially the advantage of being 15 years in the same company, obviously you know the business structure very well. You know your business associates very well too, and you know the business strategy, and you develop your business strategy. So, yes, I will say that I am very comfortable.' She also recognized that she had additional challenges because of the portfolios she was carrying. Similarly a Managing Director in Hong Kong, looked ahead to the further success of the company and identified herself closely with that success: 'What I'd really like to see, maybe five, ten years down the road, that the company ... can be listed, that it will be profitable enough to be listed in the stock exchange. That is what I would like to see or be a major business aircraft manager in the company in Hong Kong or China.'

The final area that defined this area of career opportunities and organizational constraints was the identification of factors that assisted career development. A Professor at the University of Hong Kong identified her ability to write academically and internationally. She had little time for those that felt in writing for a local market they had lost out in the promotion stakes. As she commented:

> ... yes there is a need to create a local literature and if you wish to reach out to most local women, you need to do it in Chinese. That's a perfectly legitimate activity. Unfortunately it will not enhance your academic career. But there's nothing to stop you doing both. I've published internationally on women in Hong Kong and women in China. I've also published locally, admittedly in English. I really don't think that arguing that Hong Kong issues are so localized to be able to attract international interest is a sufficient reason for saying that you don't get published internationally. I don't believe it to be true, I think it depends on the quality of the research or the thinking that's embodied in what you write.

A Chair Professor in Medicine in Hong Kong felt that she had never been very goal oriented, rather process oriented and that this was a factor in assisting her career advancement, she had simply enjoyed the work and not focused on the rewards *per se.* By contrast a Senior Vice-President for a company in Singapore maintained that it was a combination of factors including being single, having the support of her family, and having drive and persistence to pursue her goals. I asked her whether she had always had this drive, her response was as follows: 'I think I have this winning spirit and I did not realize it until later ... I like to win so much, when I was in school, I was always first in my class and even when I reached this level, I will go to the next level ... so when you hit on a target, you always want to go and climb the next higher mountain. So I think I have that, a love of that kind of winning spirit.'

In Hong Kong, a Senior Lecturer in Law felt that the single most significant factor which assisted her career advancement was her work with Anna Wu on the Equal

Opportunities Bill because she had the opportunity to get involved in a legislative project: 'Up until then I was always on the outside writing to government on behalf of women's organizations, pleading with government to do something. But once Anna Wu took on that project, I was able to work on the inside in many ways. Not inside government, but inside the legislature.' Interestingly a political opinion-leader in Hong Kong did not define her invitation to join the Legislative Council in Hong Kong as the single most significant factor in her career advancement, in fact she pointed to a gender issue as the most significant factor – being a woman: 'I think for me it was definitely an advantage. It was an advantage, because I was obviously different. Sometimes people didn't regard me as a direct competitor, because I was a woman. People were willing to let me do things, instead of giving the job to a guy whom they felt was competition.'

Conclusion

The relationship between gender and segmented labour markets in a number of global cities in Asia is, as Castells (1996) has shown, frequently driven by state imperatives including the nationalist project of the developmental state. The relationship between gender equity and organizational constraints is one fundamentally related to state politics in global cities such as Hong Kong and Singapore. This chapter has reviewed a number of different areas in relation to gender equity and organizational constraints including: issues of equal opportunities as both policy and practice; gender politics in the organization; promotion and career aspirations; and factors assisting or hampering career development.

Chapter 4

Leadership and Management Issues
for Professional Women
in Organizational Structures

Leadership and management are now centrally important issues in both corporate and academic life. The corporate restructuring of universities in the 1990s has resulted in the 'bottom line' being as significant a variable in academic as in corporate thinking. The language of the market and the global economy reached its peak in the 1990s with the emergence of the global knowledge economy as the motivating force for both academic and corporate life, and the designation of academics among others as 'knowledge workers' (Jones, 2000; Brooks, 2001). The language of business, corporate life and education fused in a way which redefined the nature of academic life, and which left many academics redefining their roles and identities (see Blackmore and Sacks, 2001). Others saw in the growth of new technologies and the 'new managerialism' the opportunity for women to break through into management and leadership in a way that had previously been denied them. The corporate downsizing of academia and the increasingly harsh competitive environment in which academics operate has shown that no breakthrough for women in management has occurred (see Ramsay, 2001). Some now see the corporate world offering more rewards and satisfaction to women who managed to break through 'the glass ceiling'. In addition senior academic women increasingly find themselves confronted by a new corporate male managerialism that translates, not only the language of management and leadership in academia, but also the nature of knowledge itself (Brooks, 2001). This chapter considers the significance of women in management and leadership and considers how women understand their position within different organizational contexts. Organizational change frequently follows legislative and policy changes and the direction of such debates is highly significant for the future growth of global cities such as Hong Kong and Singapore and the positioning of women in these debates.

In any analysis of organizational factors that could promote the advancement of women into positions of management and leadership, changing attitudes is seen as a crucial factor in assisting women move into positions of leadership. A Professor at the University of Hong Kong related changing attitudes to an understanding of equal opportunities:

... it is a fiercely difficult job, and, its not as though you are dealing with people who have been trained for management, then you would be dealing with people who have been introduced to ideas about gender equality, equal opportunities, not just gender, but race and disability, from the earliest days of their first degree. But you're not dealing with those sorts of people in senior management in a university. I mean if you leave aside the administration, technically anyway, university managers are supposed to be academics but they come from a hugely diverse range of backgrounds. They've never had management training. They may well be specialists in their own area, but being a specialist in electronic engineering, doesn't tell you anything about equal opportunity management policies. I find it difficult to know how attitudes can be changed, when there's no obviously accessible points where you can enter into an environment where there are large numbers of people whose ideas you can influence, who are going to go on to be university managers.

These views are absolutely central in highlighting deficiencies within organizational structures and management training. Issues of equity or even ethics are rarely seen as important components of management training. Managers are generally in positions because of their willingness to hold such positions and not because of any aptitude to handle management issues at a higher level.

An Associate Professor at a university in Singapore saw gender and gender issues as a fundamental factor impacting on women in organizations, and as with the Professor at the University of Hong Kong, her question is: 'How does one incorporate gender issues into organizational culture?' She commented as follows:

I think first and foremost, is the recognition that there are gender differences, and that gender differences are not going to go away. And by pretending that they are not there or penalizing women because they are there, has become a burden for women in organizations. So how does one incorporate that aspect into organizations? I think Hewlett Packard is an example of an organization that we should bear in mind. The CEO of Hewlett Packard, when his children were nine and seven or thereabouts ... his wife died, I think of cancer. And he, in effect, became a working mother. Most women who experience that cannot talk about it, or bring it into an organizational framework, but he could. And once he recognized what it entailed he devised a whole lot of policies that were gender friendly. So I would argue for 'a different way of talking' ... you need to really bring gender issues to the forefront and make it a real aspect of organizational behaviour.

She went on to say how a woman manager/leader is caught in a very difficult situation:

... if a woman in a managerial position brings in gender issues, then she is suddenly seen as this woman bringing in nonsensical ideas ... issues that are then dismissed by the organization as not germane problems. So I see how it took a man to do it. Precisely because he is a male he has greater legitimacy to bring it out into the open without being accused of taking a ridiculous position.

A Research Fellow from a Research Institute in Singapore saw having different models of leadership as being the crucial issue which would allow greater mobility into leadership for both women (and men), with different styles of leadership. As she commented:

> You see, right now, leadership is defined as being very decisive, very authoritative, you have all the facts, and this is the way it is. And when you manage as a leader ... your goals are everything, you have to get it done, that sort of thing. But there's another type of leadership which is facilitative ... more a question of saying, let's get the best out of each person, you know let's see how things can be done, as opposed to what needs to be done. I'm sure there are many other forms of leadership, which, if we went away and thought about it, we could come up with. So that we allow for a greater diversity in models of leadership ... and hence I'm sure that gender-bias that women ... 'fluff' around a lot, that sort of thing, will be seen as a strength. That it's not 'fluffing around', but its actually caring for the relationships that are involved in the organization.

She saw this model as extending not just to debates about women in the workplace, needing childcare facilities, but extending the debate to issues around '"active citizenship", so that the form of the dialogue changes from one of instrumentalism to one of facilitation'. She also made an interesting point about benchmarking when it came to organizations like research units, which have a very flat structure when it came to promotion and career advancement. She felt that while other academic organizations, like universities, assessed performance on internationally referred journals and research funding, she felt that time spent at a research unit would be difficult to assess and benchmark. This was a limitation, she felt, to more people joining the organization and she felt that Singapore itself had a very small research agenda and this was also a limitation for those interested in researching further afield.

A Senior Research Fellow in Singapore saw the issue of 'family-friendly firms' and support structures in the workplace as an important policy factor in creating organizational structures more supportive of women. She felt that the Singapore government was putting a lot of effort into promoting family-friendly firms. I asked her if she thought the policy was directed more towards domestic firms than towards multi-national companies in Singapore. She thought that it was a general policy but she thought, at least on the face of it, that multi-nationals were more advanced in terms of being family-friendly than smaller companies. She thought this was understandable because smaller firms do not have as much flexibility in terms of allocation of resources. I asked her in what ways she thought multi-nationals were more family friendly, she said that the multi-nationals have for ages operated a five day week, whereas in Singapore, most organizations operate a five and a half day week. This clearly means employees of multi-nationals have more time to spend with their families compared with employees of local companies.

Research shows that when women reach the top of organizational structures, they are usually quite exceptional, whereas it appears men in equivalent positions can often appear very mediocre and generally unexceptional. I reflected on these issues with a Chair-Professor in Medicine in Hong Kong, on what she thought about exceptional women getting to the top. She felt that provided women were very good in their field, they would make it to the top. I disagreed with her position maintaining that women frequently do not make it to the top because of a range of organizational constraints and processes of discrimination, and that men who made it to the top were certainly far from exceptional.

Promoting the Concept of Women in Leadership

Legislation is also a significant factor in defining change. While legislation in itself will not change attitudes, it does provide an opportunity to test potentially discriminatory attitudes in the courts. As Petersen (1996) notes, as a result of the political and legal changes that occurred during the transition to 1997, 'Citizens of Hong Kong developed a greater awareness of human rights issues and women have successfully identified equality as a "human right" deserving legal protection.' A Senior Lecturer in Law having been involved in policy and legislative issues concerning anti-discrimination and equal opportunities, discussed the issue of whether the University of Hong Kong, which she had direct experience of, promotes the concept of women in leadership. Her response was as follows:

> I don't think it promotes it at all. I think it tolerates it, if women comply with their idea of what success is. One thing that I would say of the University of Hong Kong, and it does hurt women, is that I think there is a tendency sometimes by department heads to dump certain administrative work on women. And I think women are not as protective of their research turf as men are. Many women do have a hard time saying 'No', to the department heads and as a result they may wind up getting more admin and less publications. However I do not want to generalize too much because there are a lot of really hard working men in our organization, and there are some women who do very little. But I do think that is one thing that hurts women at the University of Hong Kong. We do have some women leaders at the University of Hong Kong, we've got some women deans, and we've got some who are chair-professors. But most of them do not appear to be concerned about other women becoming leaders. Cecilia Chan [Dean of the Faculty of Social Sciences] is one of those rare exceptions. It is a concern of hers. She wants more women to get promoted and she often talks about strategies for getting more women promoted.

I asked what additional factors would assist women to move into positions of leadership at the University of Hong Kong. She thought that if there was an explicit policy of giving more credit to administrative responsibility and teaching, that would help. She indicated that the University of Hong Kong has been paying lip service to that recently: '... but I don't think it is policy yet, at least not generally in the university. I think many women have sacrificed their research a bit, to be a good citizen in the department ... I think there are women who feel that in the end they didn't get the credit they were expecting, and they should have protected their turf more and just published.'

So how do women leaders and managers in the corporate and academic world define themselves, their work identities, and their attitudes to leadership and management in the new millennium? Women addressed these, and other questions, and produced challenging and interesting responses. Their views are set out in this chapter. Issues include how they define their priorities as a manager in the organization, identifying qualities of women in positions of leadership, considering whether women bring different qualities to the managerial role to men, assessing to what extent they define themselves as a leader in the organization (and on what basis), distinguishing between a woman manager and a woman in a leadership role, identifying women role models in the organization, considering whether women managers are expected to behave in the same way as male managers, or whether they are expected to define a different managerial style, and considering whether the organization they are part of promotes the concept of women in leadership and management. Women in management and leadership in corporate life in Asia have traditionally confronted a number of issues regarding their position as leaders and managers. The findings of this research extend, amplify, and qualify existing research on women in management and leadership and organizational change in Asia.

Identifying Priorities as a Manager in an Organization

A factor that emerged strongly from the responses to the issue of how women define priorities as a manager in the organization is the way in which senior women in both corporate and academic life saw their management role as one of facilitating team building and leadership, and in the process of being a conciliator. This emerges as a strong quality for women in management in this research. As one academic woman in Hong Kong commented, it appears to avoid the ego or 'testosterone politics' engaged in by male managers. Women managers in the corporate world saw people as human capital, intrinsic to the success of the organization, so people development was an important factor in their people management. A Managing Director of a company in Hong Kong outlined the position clearly: 'My priority is to develop my people, and building profits for the company by developing your people, developing them to the next level. I think in our business, or in any business, people are always the major asset in our company.' A Senior Vice-President of a company in Singapore held a similar view. She commented:

> My priorities are the setting out of a set of objectives for, in this case, the business unit to achieve and to communicate this to all the people, so that everyone moves in the same direction. At the same time to manage people in order to achieve the results, because I firmly believe that it is the people who achieve the results for the company, rather than me as an individual. I only have 24 hours in one day, so there is only so much I can do, but if I can get five people to put in the same amount of effort, I can achieve better results, people development is one of the key priorities in the organization.

When asked about the potential for conflict among executive peers and how this is dealt with, her response was as follows:

> It depends on the frequency of differences, if the frequency is relatively little I think we can compromise, and give and take. But if it is so often that the decision making is

always different from your bosses or peers, then I think you ought to revisit the fit in the organization. So far as this is concerned, I don't have this difficulty but there are always some cases where you feel so strongly that you are right and that the decision that was made was not in favour of your position, I usually go after the meeting is over, on a one to one with my boss, and say that something is missing in that other decision, and ask if we can look at the case again and come to some agreement and then we re-invite the rest of the team to open up the case again.

Women in management in academic life also showed the same pattern of team building, listening and being a conciliator, as women in corporate life, while retaining a decision making position. A Deputy Head of Department at a university in Singapore said that her style on management was very accommodative, and that she used networking a lot and spent a lot of time talking with people, and just trying to understand how we can fit people in, so that we can achieve the objectives of the organization. When asked if she saw herself as a leader in decision making, she indicated that she saw herself as giving people opportunities to actually contribute to decision making, but eventually she would probably have to make the decision herself. I asked a Chair Professor in Medicine in Hong Kong if she saw herself as a leader within the academic and medical communities in Hong Kong. She responded as follows: 'I don't see myself as a leader in a traditional sense, but I see myself as being able to work with people and getting things done ... to get them to think or feel that they did that, rather than saying I did that for everybody.' A Senior Programme Director at the University of Hong Kong, also prioritized working within a team:

> ... as a priority I like to think, why am I here, how can I do it better. Not the nitty-gritties ... but how can I make this product more meaningful to the consumer. So for me, that is an absolute priority. The second priority, which must be damn close behind that, is having everybody come along with me. So it's very important for me to feel like I have communicated the message to people around me. So those are my two priorities I need to have a sense of accomplishment ... and I need to have a sense of collegiality and accomplishment with the people I'm working with.

Both the Chair Professor in Medicine in Hong Kong and a Senior Lecturer in Law at the University of Hong Kong gave priority to developing and working with people, human resources development, having good people, trusting them, and giving them responsibilities, were all identified as important.

A Senior Academic Administrator in Singapore prioritized structural change within the organization, which positioned people in a very different way:

> ... a large part of it would have to be putting in place certain structures, and divorcing people from positions as such. Putting in place certain structures where a system could work regardless of who was there ... so that things would be able to continue and have a system that is fair and above board and as transparent as much as it can be.

A Research Fellow in Singapore whose work demanded strict time constraints, prioritized research outcomes:

Managing, as in driving the research agenda and its outcomes in terms of a timeframe that makes it relevant … you don't want to drive it for so long so that it is no longer relevant. So time is important. Secondly, it's got to be delivered in a way that is accessible to your audience, so that's another important criteria. Third, most of what we have to do also requires that you show that views are representative.

Beyond the identification of similarities in how many senior women in academic and corporate life identified priorities in the organization, a broader question they were asked to consider was: do women bring different qualities to the managerial role from men and, if so, what are these qualities? Some of the positive qualities women were identified as having included: being more consultative, democratic, persuasive, patient, understanding, altruistic, conscientious, reliable, accessible and in addition, as having more depth of perception and more energy. Negatives attributed to women managers included: 'being temperamental', petty, too emotional, rigid. It is always difficult to avoid stereotypes, although some women did draw on stereotypical models, others while cautious of generalizations, made perceptive comments.

Women Bringing Different Qualities to the Managerial Role from Men

The global knowledge economy produces a new type of 'knowledge worker' and demands a new kind of management style. This was recognized by a Senior Academic Administrator at the National University of Singapore who made the following comments:

At the risk of generalization, I think women tend to be more consultative. I think women tend to be more democratic in position … Whereas, I've noticed that men tend to be more, perhaps assertive, if you like, more command and control … Of course there may be exceptions … I think this is an important quality for a knowledge based economy. Because if you're dealing with knowledge workers, then you really need to let them express themselves, and hear their views. Even though you may not agree, to really get the best from them, the best ideas.

Another Senior Academic Administrator in Singapore related the situation more to her personal experience:

I think men tend … to be very much more assertive in their leadership roles … I experienced a very different leader in my predecessor, and I do things very differently … a lot more persuasion, a lot more sitting down and explaining things, which as you pointed out, can be a lot more time consuming … Sometimes I wish I had a little bit more male in me, in terms of just saying … I've heard the views, I hear the unhappiness, let's talk about it some more. I think that's where I need a little bit more of a learning curve, and I probably sound like a classic case of a woman wanting to be more like a man.

Women in senior positions in the corporate and academic world shared the idea of women being more meticulous and paying more attention to detail. A Dean at the University of Hong Kong had the following perspective:

Because there are so few women in managerial positions, its difficult to generalize, but I would say generally women are more conscientious. Women are more selfless. Women look at the organization from an overall benefit, and less so from self interest. They are more altruistic. The reason I say this is because if you look at civil servants in Hong Kong, people are saying that women are becoming so important, and all the bureau chiefs and department heads are women. Actually it is about 30 percent, only one third. Why is it possible ... because most of the top level civil servants, who are male, have left for private companies, and they earn salaries, double, triple, quadruple, immediately. Women did not venture into these jobs because women are better at housekeeping, and we are not aggressive in developing and forging personal careers, hence women like organizations like the university, and like the civil service structure. Women are more reliable I would say, more trustworthy, because our tendency is to look at the collective interest. Because as mothers, as housewives, we look to family, we take the collective interest prior to our self interest. The mentality is more nurturing and protective than men who may take this as a stepping stone for their own career advancement ... my general impression.

A Senior Vice-President in the corporate world in Singapore made a similar point: 'I think women tend to be more meticulous, something which I feel would be good in the area of planning. I think women are good at putting things down, planning and seeing to its execution ... Women generally have more patience, to see to the final results ... these are some of the qualities I see in women.' A Managing Director of a company in Hong Kong saw women in the business world as being more inclusive: 'Yes, I definitely believe there's a fundamental difference between men and women. And I have found business women tend to be a little more comprehensive than men. Men tend to look at the bigger picture and don't like to focus on little things ... But women tend to be much more comprehensive and more thorough.'

A Senior Programme Director at the University of Hong Kong saw the difference between women and men managers as being quite stark:

Absolutely, I think we've got a depth of perception. Men seem to be much more instrumental, in my observation, and certainly in my experience here. I have certainly worked for two guys with vision, and these two men have certainly influenced my approach to my career. But on the whole, I find that men ... are much more interested in setting up structures, setting up information systems, to get to the ... bottom lines, and have less concern about making sure we're all on the same page. So I think women bring a depth to the role, in my experience. Another thing, frankly, that women bring, that I find men don't, and that's energy. I don't know where we get it from because we have to expend it in many different directions. But women in work are so much more energized. Certainly in this institution, no doubt about it. The men here are, nearly half-way to the grave, relative to the energies and enthusiasms that women have. Women are also much more perceptive in a broader field. So they'll bring experiences to a problem, then go outside the realm of what men do.

A Professor at the University of Hong Kong also saw women as being much more accessible in a managerial context to men:

I feel that my experience is limited. I'm speaking only from my experience, then I would say that men are emotionally inaccessible, more remote, and far more mechanical in their approach to management. They're much more given to producing formulae for the allocation of work for instance. Women are more accessible. I think they're better managers of the kind of human emotion side of management ... So, just based on that experience of comparing emotionally constipated males with women, who are much more accessible, outgoing.

There were some negatives seen as associated with women managers and leaders. A Senior Educational Administrator for the legal profession in Hong Kong had some of the following reservations:

... I know some women who very deliberately model themselves on males, in order to become what they see as a more effective manager ... I've found, it may just be my experience, and obviously that's all I can talk from. But I have found generally that men are more understanding and less difficult ... less personal perhaps, and less rigid. Whereas female bosses tend to be more rigid, and very much time watchers, and just not such pleasant people to work for at all. But ... I haven't worked with a great many people, so I don't think too much emphasis should be put on my answer ... Let me just add something to that. I think women are very good managers. I think being a good manager and being a good boss are two entirely different things. I think women are very good managers because they spend a lot of their lives managing. They do far more management; even a housewife probably does more managing than a man does, in juggling various roles. And they're very good ... at doing a large number of things at once ... But as bosses, [women are] I think less understanding ... Maybe its because they are trying to prove that they are better than men ... I don't know.

A Managing Director in Hong Kong also had some very definite views about women managers: 'Now however, I have also found that women tend to be more petty in terms that can be construed as being nasty, sometimes. Because we tend to pick up on little issues a lot of times.' She found that women tended to be more emotional than men, and she felt that the emotional part of the female tends to come out in how we deal with business:

I'm sure you've read the book *Men are from Mars and Women are from Venus.* We tend to be much more emotional in the way we do things; in a professional capacity or even in a personal relationship ... I have been around women who have those kinds of traits. Some women are much more aware of their shortcomings, and they try to change them, but there are some women who are not, and they can be viewed by our male partners as being too emotional or not grown up in some ways.

While women are also seen as being more compassionate, more understanding, and gaining more satisfaction from people, a Director of a Research Unit in Singapore, while acknowledging the difficulty of generalizing, saw women in management as paying greater attention to detail, having more patience, and deriving more satisfaction from people, rather than tasks. A Deputy Director of a Research Unit in Singapore felt that: '... women tend to be more understanding about familial roles, and are more compassionate.' However, like the Managing Director in Hong Kong, this Deputy Director indicated that women could be more petty. This depth of interest on the part of women managers was often seen as in contrast with that of the instrumentalism of male managers.

An Associate Professor from a university in Singapore deepened the analysis by reflecting the issues through the lens of gender analysis. As she commented:

> ... within organizations, often promotion is dependent on you being able to do a piece of work in relation to certain kinds of characteristics, which really actually favour the masculine over the feminine. So very often, women in positions of power, women in positions of seniority, have had to learn the knowledge, the skills and so on of the masculine. And actually sometimes in a very concerted way, even minimize the feminine qualities that could actually be an advantage. But for those women who are consciously aware ... that feminine qualities may be an advantage ... they do bring something quite different to the organization.

A Chair-Professor in Medicine in Hong Kong summed up the situation of women as managers and leaders: 'Women are more process oriented ... and I think women are definitely more sensitive to people's needs ... success or failure is not the end of the world. I mean failure is not the end of the world. Women can take failure better than men. And women can walk away from failure better than men.'

Qualities of a Woman in a Leadership Role

The issue of what are the qualities of a woman in a leadership role revealed, perhaps not unexpectedly, a consideration of the relationship between gender and leadership. There was an interesting division between those who took the position that gender should not be a factor in leadership, and who offered best practice models of leadership, and those who offered a more realistic assessment of gender and leadership within organizations. Both a Senior Academic Administrator and a Senior Research Fellow in Singapore fell into the first category, arguing that gender should not be a factor in leadership, arguing that the qualities of leadership should be gender-neutral. By contrast a gender analysis was given by two other women also writing out of a Singapore experience. A Deputy Director of a Research Unit at a university in Singapore stated that a woman leader should: 'Fight for less discrimination against women in organizational settings.' An Associate Professor at a university in Singapore highlighted some of the benefits that women leaders can bring to any organization:

> ... a woman can bring in perspectives that would otherwise be missing, and not taken into consideration in drawing up policies, programmes and so on. I will just mention one of them, if you leave gender out of organizations, when actually it is very much present, then how do you design, say promotional prospects and career advancement ... And so that perspective itself, the ability to see that as a genuine perspective, a perspective that is legitimate, that needs to be brought into the forefront of things.

Women interviewed in Hong Kong had no illusions about the gender politics operating within institutions and how this impacts on women leaders. A Senior Programme Director in Hong Kong laid out the politics of women in leadership:

> I think the woman would have to have enormous academic ability, again the energy issue is a huge one, because we have to multi-task. But I think, really, sadly, she has to have manipulative skills, and I distinguish that from facilitative skills. I've recognized that I am not manipulative enough, aggressive enough in my facilitation. Yes, I get things done with people, but when I meet an obstacle … I don't know how to manage that. Well … I do know how to manage it, but I personally don't want to engage in those tactics. So in a sense, unfortunately, you have to have a micro-political bent, and I am not good with that … I believe that women need to have steel in their spine to keep them from bending under the pressures. Because I'm a softie, I have to admit it, relative to all sorts of piercing self-confidence that you need to have.

A Professor at the University of Hong Kong framed her analysis in the context of a woman leader, a chair-professor (who had left the university), who, she felt had many of the qualities which made her very successful in the role of leader/manager:

> As a chair-professor, you don't have much choice, you have to take up management positions within the university, you have to chair university committees. (Name of chair professor) was very good at conflict-resolution, she did not let herself get involved. There was none of this 'horn-locking' that you see with males, where the substantive position under discussion becomes subsidiary to their testosterone level. (Name of chair-professor) was given some of the most difficult committees to deal with, and she appeared to deal with them very fruitfully. And I think it was partly because she didn't get involved in these males games. Some men found her very difficult to handle, because she was a strong woman, and she was also physically big. She was nearly six foot tall, and she had a large frame, so she was quite imposing. But she was very able, both academically speaking, and in terms of management. Now, she would be my ideal of a very competent female manager who hasn't lost her female abilities, whatever they are, and however we name them, and who survived quite well in a predominantly male world at the chair-professor and higher level.

The issue of leadership is frequently not an easy one to define and the concepts of leadership and management are frequently used interchangeably. In addition, leadership is frequently seen as an attribute held by individuals, or something individuals feel they themselves have, rather than a formal position or title. Leadership is frequently distinguished from management by a distinction that attributes management as having an instrumental quality, and leadership as having a visionary quality. To be successful, leadership does require the support and confidence of individuals, management does not necessarily require either, although this does help the process of management. The research findings show that women are sometimes reluctant leaders, or in some cases found leadership thrust upon them, by default. In other cases, some women thrive on the support and encouragement of their peers to be a leader, even though the organization concerned may only consider them leaders in a most informal sense. Some women who hold management positions understand their role to be one of leadership, even if the process of leadership may not be successful to anyone but the person concerned. Leadership is about bringing through decisions that are regarded as successful for the organization, and supported by staff, an almost irreconcilable situation in many cases.

Women in this research were asked to what extent they defined themselves as a leader in the organization. The following three perspectives, while very different, had in common the strategic nature of leadership, whether for the benefit of the organization, or more generally for the good of a specific community of interests. A Senior Academic Administrator at the National University of Singapore defined herself as someone who is able to give a vision, and who reminded people which direction the university is going in, and to motivate them to share this vision and bring it to fruition. As she indicated this is what leadership is about, and it is not easy. An Associate Professor from a university in Singapore saw her role as a leader in speaking up on any significant issues that emerged within a social, political or organizational context. A Senior Vice-President of a company in Singapore saw leadership as being strategically important in business meetings:

> ... usually when I go to a meeting, the objective of the meeting is always set out in your mind, you think that I am going to the meeting to achieve a set of objectives, and how you steer the meeting to achieve the objectives is a very important factor because everyone will have their own agenda in the meeting, so if you do not set your direction accordingly, or steer the meeting to your agenda, then you end up achieving nothing in the meeting.

The issue around whether leadership is something defined within a specific position, or a quality, was shown in the views of two academic women in Hong Kong, one who held a very senior position in the organization, and who was known as an innovator, and agent of change, and the second, who occupied a less senior position, but saw herself, and was seen by others, as a leader. Both clearly defined leadership as quite distinct from management, both saw themselves as acting as a conscience of the organization and both were involved in giving students a voice within the organization. I asked a Dean from the University of Hong Kong to what extent she defined herself as a leader; she had already defined herself as an advocate for entrepreneurial change. She responded by saying that she was a good mobilizer of people, and of making them recognize grievances and then collectively making use of that. She indicated that:

> ... we actually changed [university] policy when everybody said it was impossible to change. I can do it gently, without bringing about too much unhappiness. I'm idealistic ... I always want for myself and my students to be able to act as a social conscience. So my unique contribution as Dean would be, I bring in students' interests, and I emphasize an overall educational objective of the university, the university's contribution to the community ... So I see myself as reinforcing the social responsibilities of the university in that sense. And I'm very proud of myself being able to do that.

A Senior Programme Director at the University of Hong Kong responded to the question of leadership as follows:

I actually think I am a leader in this organization. I don't need the organization to tell me so. I know that people respect my opinions, they seek me out and I know that the students get endorsements obviously. I also get lots of criticisms, but that's good, I'm happy enough that that happens. I do think I have a sense of what this organization ought to be doing. Whether I translate this into results is obviously up to them to judge. But I do believe I get results as well. So I perceive leadership as something very different from management. I don't think they're necessarily interchangeable. I think you have to have qualities of managerial ability in a leadership role. But I don't think you need to be a leader to be a manager at all.

A Managing Director of a company in Hong Kong saw herself as leading by example: 'I like to lead by example, that's my style. I don't like to dictate. I like to bring out the potential from my managers, so I like to direct them rather than dictate, in pointing them in the right direction. Or sometimes when I know that they probably know a lot better than I do, I let them take the leading role in that situation.

Some women, seen as leaders, did not want to 'carry the mantle', a Senior Lecturer in Law did not see herself as a leader and did not want to be: '... mainly because I think it will prevent me from being what I want to be, which is a leader in research'. A Chair-Professor in Medicine in Hong Kong said that she had never consciously fulfilled the role of leader so she was always at a loss when people called her a leader: 'I've never consciously thought about it or consciously worked towards it.' I asked her about having vision, and whether she felt she had convinced people to support that vision. She responded as follows:

Yes, but not in any sort of proselytizing way. I never go and hard sell, it's usually by example and initially by discussion. That's the one thing I love. I generate ideas as I talk to people, I find it much, much easier and even when I talk to my personal assistant, who is much younger, I just toss issues around and eventually both of us will come out with a solution, or a way of tackling the problem or a way of packaging the issue.

I asked this Chair-Professor how she gets her views across, and whether she ever has to fight to get her views accepted. Her response is as follows:

I don't fight, so the way I do things ... now that you've asked me ... I have this idea, or if people don't accept it, then I think okay, its an academic exercise. I've reached this point, its intellectually stimulating, fine and next time around I bring up some ideas, eventually the time is right for the idea to develop, then people will take it. So it's not painful, it's not an effort. For instance, I think this is a very good example, for many years, when I was in medical school, we thought that one of the most important things was doctor/patient relationships and that doctors should be able to have a dialogue with patients. Now the Hong Kong environment was totally unaccepting of the idea, it wasn't ready. At the time I fought hard to have communication skills, interpersonal skills entered into the curriculum, it would come to nothing, I just got my nose bloody ... then 'bang', the hospital authority came in with a mission statement of patient-centred care, with people suing doctors all over the place. The media blowing up all sorts of things about doctors. Then the time was ready for this idea to come in. And then we had curriculum reform, so there was a lot of curriculum time available for what the faculty considered as worthwhile topics and courses. So that's when I introduced the whole clinical and interpersonal skills.

Women Leaders Changing Corporate Culture

A political 'opinion-leader' experience of working as a commodities trader for a multi-national corporation was outlined earlier. Her success and emphasis on communication skills saw her move into a position of Regional Managing Director. She set about, in her role as manager/leader, trying to change male Chinese corporate culture through creating a more interactive work environment and was confronted by a number of obstacles.

> When I became Regional Managing Director I tried to do something that everybody wanted when we were employees. Before I was boss, we always discussed among ourselves the things we wished our bosses would do, like seek our opinion. And as commodities traders we're paid a huge bonus. The bonus is supposed to reflect our P&L (profit and loss) performance. This is a very important moment for traders, for people in our business, sometimes we don't know why we were given so much or so little and we always say, I wish they would talk with us ... So when I became the Managing Director, the first thing I said was we're going to talk about the annual bonus before I make the recommendations to the US.

Her attempts at creating a more interactive environment and one where there was greater transparency in its operation ran into challenges from older Chinese men. Some of the older Asian men had problems with her new style of management as she noted:

> They bitched about it when we were colleagues, but once I became boss, one of the older very experienced men said: 'I just can't talk to you about money'. I said: 'What do you mean you can't talk about money, we've known each other for years' and he said: 'I just don't know how to do it, I've never done it, I know you'll do your best for me.' It took me three years to get this man to feel comfortable to talk about his performance and money ... I was trying to change the culture, the corporate culture. I spent a lot of time doing that sort of thing.

Given her dual leadership role in the corporate world and in politics, I asked her if the nature of leadership changed in both arenas, for example she was clearly a team leader in the corporate world, was she also a team leader politically or did she see herself as an individual defining the direction of policy? Her response was as follows:

> I feel very much a lone voice in politics. But then I realize that perhaps my role is to articulate those concerns. At the time that I got into politics I felt that the 'environment' didn't get the light of day. The other thing that I did in my bizcareer was that I built an entirely new market analysis system. I'm sort of a systems builder. I believe in using

experience, intuition, and facts and stir-fry and see what you get out of it. I was brought up with a Socratic education where we sat down and deliberated and debated issues.

As regards women role models, many of the women interviewed had difficulties identifying women, who they felt represented role models for women in leadership and management. A Dean at the University of Hong Kong said that she could not think of a role model: 'Let me give the reason why, no. It's because we have no woman vice-chancellor, no woman pro-vice chancellor, no woman dean until recently, no senior staff in chair-professor positions who are women. So there's just no woman around who can act as our role models ... just men. It isn't that women can't act as role models.' A Research Fellow in Singapore saw the [now ex-] Director of a research unit as having a role model profile:

> She does deliver and deliver very well. She's the superlative type person in the Singapore establishment, so she's quite a role model. But she's also very sharp, intelligent, I mean, you can't put anything past her. So that's good for me, because I'm usually very willing to accommodate, well you know you can have your view, and I can have mine. But, for her, there's a right view and a wrong view, and these are the reasons why.

In Hong Kong a range of women 'opinion-leaders' were identified as role models, a Senior Lecturer in Law saw Anna Wu as a role model:

> She's not that much older than me and I think she's been a very good model for me in the sense that she's very committed to her goals and her values. But she is good at understanding the other side, and working with the other side ... She's good at building bridges, seeing the other point of view. Which is important, I think.

A Senior Educational Administrator for the legal profession in Hong Kong saw the legal profession as having a number of women role models:

> ... there's certainly several women who are role models for barristers, several highly successful senior counsel ... Audrey Yu [Senior Counsel] is one ... she is a very successful barrister. She is also standing for election for Hong Kong Island to the Legislative Council ... She's excellent. There's also Margaret Ng, again a barrister, standing for the Legal Constituency in the Legislative Council. There's Jacqueline Leong [Senior Counsel] who is an excellent barrister ... I mean those three come to mind and they have also been leaders of the Bar Council in the recent past.

A Managing Director in Hong Kong indicated: 'The woman that I really aspire to is a person like Anson Chan, I really think that she has a very balanced life, and she is a great leader.'

So are women in management and leadership expected to behave in the same way as male managers, or are they expected to have a different style of leadership? A Professor at the University of Hong Kong saw women as having had little choice historically as regards their management style:

I think historically they are supposed to adopt male management styles. If a woman historically has achieved a management position at the University of Hong Kong, I think that the system deals with that by encouraging, structuring, shaping that female into a male like person … I'm thinking back on all the female heads or senior staff, I've known. I can't really think of any of them who have clearly brought a female quality into the leadership … and its not meant in any condemnatory way, they've had to basically play the game as its played, or they're not in the game.

This professor went on to say how few positions of leadership existed for women at the University of Hong Kong. She noted that in over twenty years, the university had only recently appointed its first female dean. The figures suggest that women at chair-professor level are rare and mostly in the medical faculty. A Chair-Professor in Medicine in Hong Kong felt that: '… modern day management is more suitable for women, and women shouldn't really behave like men. Now the management structure is more flat, it's more egalitarian and women are in fact more suitable to those roles … It's the wrong time to be like a man.' A Deputy Director of a Research Unit in Singapore maintained that: 'Male managers expect women to behave like men but women leaders have never shared that expectation, and will sing their own tune.' An Associate Professor at a university in Singapore outlined what she saw as the gender politics involved in expected behaviour patterns for male and female managers:

I think women managers are in an incredibly delicate position. In the first place, if they behave in the way male managers do, then for example their assertiveness may be seen as aggressiveness. Their demand for certain kinds of standards may be seen as, you know, that she's acting bossy, she's not being fair. So on the one hand there is the perception that, and in fact some people say, I'd rather have a male boss than a woman boss because they are worse. And I think this is because of the behavior of male managers, because its not seen as appropriate behaviour for women to take on, and they will be judged harshly. Similarly if they are emotional then they are not as good, they can't make rational decisions, they are behaving like a woman … It's just, you know, damned if you do, damned if you don't kind of position, that you are put into.

Conclusion

The issue of management and leadership is clearly one which is gender related and defined at least in part by the gendered nature of organizations. The findings of this research highlight the paucity of women managers and leaders in both Singapore and Hong Kong and the lack of a range of role models. While the distinction between management and leadership was understood, there was some difference of view as to whether particular qualities could or should be attributed to women leaders. Some of the respondents felt that leadership as a concept needed to carry gender-neutral qualities. Others recognized that the gender politics operating in organizations make gender neutrality within any conception of leadership and management very difficult to sustain. Women were clearly seen as bringing a range of qualities to management including: conscientiousness, altruism, attention to detail, energy, reliability, accessibility, depth of perception, compassion and understanding. Some negatives were also associated with women managers that conformed to stereotyped perceptions including pettiness, being difficult, irrationality, and emotionality. The strategic role of women within positions of management and leadership was well understood and the politics involved, made many women decide they did not want to be involved as a result. Traditional patterns of management were seen to be more a feature of academic life than corporate life, with very few women reaching the most senior positions of leadership and management in academia. Few women defined distinctively new types of management or leadership style, or seemed to have any experience of innovative management styles, despite a considerable literature on the subject. Several who had been in leadership roles for some time seemed to be somewhat unreflective about leadership style, and more concerned with dealing with matters on an issue by issue basis. It is clear that more research is needed on the development of new styles of management and leadership for professional women within organizations.

Chapter 5

Intimacy, Work and Family Life: Social and Personal Issues Confronting Professional Woman in Global Cities

Women in professional life in Hong Kong and Singapore face a number of personal and social issues that confront women in any global city undergoing rapid economic, social and political change. While Hong Kong and Singapore are international and cosmopolitan cities, having international and diverse communities, and becoming significant centres in terms of the growth of the global knowledge economy, both are also Chinese cities in terms of composition and history. While the Chinese populations in Hong Kong and Singapore are very different, and in Singapore are part of a much broader multi-ethnic mix, there are a number of traditional elements of Chinese family and business life which give these populations a particular definition, and which provide professional women with a number of additional challenges to those they confront in western societies. Hong Kong is a more open society than Singapore, where attitudes to marriage and procreation are still seen as a legitimate area of intervention for state policies. Singapore's pro-natalist policy is of course well known and is still ongoing, although increasingly challenged by a pragmatic and materialistic population, somewhat tired by such interventions into their private lives. However women in both Hong Kong and Singapore are still under pressure to get married, and being single, whether successful or not, is still a deviant activity, as is the decision not to procreate. There are also the vestiges of the traditional pattern of younger women marrying much older Chinese men. Divorce, while increasingly prevalent, is socially frowned upon and divorcees are seen as social failures in terms of marriage and procreation. This chapter explores the intersecting nexus of intimacy, work and family life confronting professional women in two global cities, Hong Kong and Singapore.

Hong Kong and Singapore are affluent cities, despite the recent recessions faced by both cities, which have already weathered the Asian economic crisis. The media in Hong Kong is focusing on the backlash against professional women in the face of the economic downturn, and directly or indirectly encouraging women to focus on family as opposed to career, putting women under increasing pressure as regards marriage partners. Professional Chinese women in Hong Kong and Singapore are being put under pressure to be less discriminating about choice of partner, and successful and well paid jobs are often portrayed negatively in terms of finding a husband as Chinese men, particularly those in Singapore, chose to marry less well educated, less successful, and women who are paid less than they are. An article, interestingly and significantly reported in *The Straits Times*, (March 10, 2002), newspaper in Singapore, entitled: 'They want to save their marriages, so ... More Guangdong women choosing life of a homemaker', reports on the 'portrayal on TV of career women whose marriages fail is sending them scurrying home'. The message is unmistakable, and reports on a survey of more than 2,000 families in a prosperous province of southern China, Guangdong, (often seen as an area in direct competition with Hong Kong) where 'the number of women holding the view that "men are social animals and women are homemakers" has risen to 60.1 percent, 17 percent higher than 10 years ago.' The article reports that in the Guangdong region women are 'bucking the trend of building career ... more Guangdong women are opting to become full-time homemakers.' The article states that social critics and feminists blame the portrayal in television drama serials for this. 'They say that images of successful career women failing to cope with their roles as wife and mother, thus driving their husbands into another woman's embrace, are the cause of the prevailing retrograde thinking among Guangdong women, *Sing Tao Daily* has reported.' Sociologist Lu Ying, from Guangzhou's Zhongshan University, who specializes in gender issues, quoted in the article, maintains that the trends suggest a revival of traditional values. The article also notes the recent amendments to marriage laws in Mainland China, which awards substantial compensation to divorced women if they have undertaken housework in their marriage. In Singapore, the anxiety among successful single women is tangible, and there is a constant stream of articles and initiatives from the Singaporean government to attempt to reduce the increasing numbers of singles, as well as childless couples. In an article which angered many successful professional single women in Singapore, a female deputy editor of the 'Life' section of *The Straits Times* newspaper, wrote an article entitled 'Be afraid, be very afraid' (April 14, 2002). Directed at single professional women in Singapore, the article went on to link fear with the loneliness of being single: 'If all else fails, perhaps the best way to get singles to marry and have babies is to drum into them the loneliness of being single and childless.' This article was followed by another heading 'Single and alone – a growing trend in the US.' A proposal in the Hong Kong legislature to cut the wages of foreign maids and thus undermine the main support structure for professional women, recently failed. The Hong Kong government announced that it will not cut the minimum wage for tens of thousands of foreign maids, despite the pressures of a recession strapped Hong Kong.

Intimacy in Asia

An article in the *Asian Wall Street Journal* (AWSJ, 2003) entitled 'The Agony and the Ecstasy' examines how issues of intimacy are surfacing in cultures traditionally associated with prudishness and repression. The article notes '"In the past, couples in Asia used to suffer in silence", says Singapore sexologist Wei Siang Yu. "Now they are talking about sexual problems ... people are talking about not having enough sex"' (AWSJ, 2003, p.1). In Hong Kong, a 2002 Chinese University of Hong Kong survey of more than 3,000 people found that 51 percent of men and 53 percent of women reported sexual problems. The article also notes that there are four sexual dysfunction clinics in Hong Kong and claims that most of the new patients are managers and executives who often have to wait a year for treatment.

In Singapore's largest sex clinic at the National University Hospital, 10 percent of couples who visit haven't yet consummated their marriages. The article quoting the head of the hospital's department of obstetrics and gynecology and president of the Asian Federation of Sexology, says that the problem is 'rampant in Asia'. He maintains that inexperience with sex before marriage and cultural myths about masturbation and ejaculation in both India and China lead many men to believe that they are born with a limited number of sperm and leave couples ill-prepared for marriage.

The Singapore sexologist, Dr Wei, maintains that the prudish veneers of many Asian countries are beginning to crumble as sex is increasingly being discussed openly. With the popularity of viagra in the Asian market, this has made sex a dinner-table topic. The article notes that in Singapore, 'the city state's low birth rate has resulted in well-publicized, government sponsored campaigns such as the Social Development's Unit online dating service and sex therapy workshops conducted by Dr Wei. In China increasing Internet access has led to a surge in the popularity of racy content such as "Passion Commune" on the Internet portal Sohu.com' (AWJS, 2003, p.4).

In Hong Kong, the article notes that the Hong Kong Family Planning Association survey on sexual trends showed that a combination of financial and work pressures have played havoc with the sexual lives of married couples in the city. In addition, the pressures resulting from high-rise living in Hong Kong and Singapore, combined with cramped living spaces with several generations under one roof make it very difficult for couples to have uninhibited sex lives.

In Singapore, Dr Wei has been working with a Singapore interior designer, to make the bedrooms of Singapore couples sexier. The pair often recommend soundproofing walls and doors as well as playing music while having sex to drown out the noise from family members. The following were based on their recommendations: 'Out went the safe that stood in the middle of the room, which kept the husband thinking about business in bed ... Out went the wife's collection of stuffed animals that also helped ruin the mood. Finally, the bed itself was redesigned. A king-sized bed may be a sign that "we've made it, we're an affluent couple", but it wasn't helping their lovemaking' (ibid.).

The Hong Kong Family Planning Association Report revealed that only 3 in 10 women were interested in sex. As one 35 year old corporate Hong Kong trainer who left her husband after 10 years, partly as a result of sexual frustrations commented: 'You read in books and watch on television all these women who are having great sexual lives, then you go to bed and its all over in five minutes,' she says. 'No wonder you get more satisfaction and gratification buying a Gucci handbag.'

The fact that Asian women are seeking greater sexual satisfaction is a key reason behind the surge in clinics catering to people with sexual problems. As the article notes, as women marry later, have sexual partners before marriage and gain greater financial independence, expectations about sex in relationships are changing. 'Dr Wei notes: "Most men use their wives as sleeping pills." Husbands are often pushed into seeking assistance for their sexual problems by their wives, "who threaten to leave them if they don't get some help," he says' (AWSJ, 2003, p.4).

Demographics and Modernization in Southeast Asia

A mixture of state interventionist policies and modernization has combined to create an interesting demographic profile in the region. Most of the Asian countries are authoritarian democracies where the nationalist agenda overshadows the gender agenda. While modernization and globalization have created a demand for more women to enter the labour force, the pressures of maintaining a middle-class way of life have forced more married women to seek paid employment. Soin (2001, p.7) notes that in 'Southeast Asia and Hong Kong most middle-class families employ maids or domestic help and this has hindered or postponed some of the negotiations over changing gender roles and responsibilities within the household.'

Another aspect of demographic change is the change in marriageable age. Women are marrying later in Singapore as a result of educational attainment and participation in the economy. Households are as a result shrinking in size and in Hong Kong women head more than twenty percent of households. In addition among older age groups more women then men are not married. In Singapore the government functions as a social strategist, Soin (2001, p.13) observes that from the 1960s, the Singapore government has used its executive and legislative power over women and the family to attain general and specific national objectives without analysis of the gender consequences. For example as a result of the declining birth rate up to the 1990s, the government proposed a selectively pro-natalist population policy encouraging couples to have three or more children. The impact of these policies are taking their toll in 2002-2003 as the government acknowledges the economic downturn and is forced to make severe cuts in the government pension fund, the Central Provident Fund (CPF).

Another aspect of state intervention is in the area of 'singlehood'. As Soin (2001, p.14) comments, the number of educated women remaining single is rising in Singapore, as in other countries. However she notes that 'the policy makers regard these educated women who reject marriage as socially unacceptable because they are not fulfilling the national objective of reproducing a "quality" population. One of the unwritten penalties for these highly educated single women is that they are perceived as unsuitable for political candidacy.' Drawing on the Census 2000, Soin highlighted two groups of people with the highest number of singles – well educated women and less educated men. She notes that 'Women with less than secondary education are two or three times more likely to marry than those with university degrees, while one in four female graduates is married to a non-graduate. Government sponsored matchmaking units have been established to help singles meet suitable partners' (Soin, 2001, p.14).

In Hong Kong, newspapers analyze how women are faring in what has become (at least as far as the media are concerned) increasingly fierce competition for men. They carry articles about why Hong Kong men seem to prefer marrying traditional mainland Chinese women and how women should lower their expectations for marriage partners. Not only is there an emphasis on the numbers of successful single women remaining single, but the stories also focus on how some female professionals make more money than their male counterparts. As Sociology Professor Odalia Wong, from Hong Kong Baptist University comments: '... in an economic downturn, people look for people to blame ... Women have become the scapegoats.' The number of Hong Kong women who remain single into their 30s and 40s has been rising for 15 years. The percentage who have never been married recently hit a new high of nearly 17 percent. This compares with an increase of single men in the same age bracket to 21 percent. As is the case with Singapore, the single professional women phenomena is seen as deviant or a social problem. Research shows that higher education levels among women have put more into professional jobs, making them financially independent. Many postpone or even give up the idea of marrying. As Hong Kong Polytechnic lecturer Catherine Ng, who is 41 and unmarried states: 'Women's level of education and economic power is much higher than in the old days. Our confidence has gone up and we're not so willing to compromise.'

Despite these pressures to conform to economic and social conventions, professional women in both Hong Kong and Singapore showed pragmatism and resilience in the face of such pressures. Purushotam (1998) claimed that middle-class women in Singapore were motivated as much by materialism, and a desire for the good life, as by ambition. In Hong Kong and Singapore salaries are high, and much higher in Hong Kong than Singapore, as is the cost of living and property, and this is clearly reflected in issues around employment and patterns of living. However in this research, professional women interviewed were talented and desired success in their careers, outside any material gain. High incomes made it possible for live-in domestic support in the form of maids, to be common in both Hong Kong and Singapore. This clearly distinguishes professional women in Hong Kong and Singapore from professional women in Europe, the US and Australasia, where live-in domestic help, with or without children is not the norm. The attitude of the Hong Kong and Singapore governments in facilitating this development has created the opportunity for many more women to reach the highest levels of corporate, political and academic life, despite organizational barriers still hampering women. Both the high incomes available, and high level of relatively low cost support services such as live-in maids, alleviated the problems faced by lack of adequate child care provided by organizations and which has been such an issue in other parts of the world. Both these factors impacted on the personal and social issues confronting professional women in Hong Kong and Singapore. However, factors which impacted on women globally, such as issues of intimacy and singlehood; marriage impacting on career decisions; issues around equity in the division of parenting and household responsibilities; familial obligations and responsibilities; and spousal attitudes to career, parenting and household, all figured as significant issues in the findings of this research.

Singlehood, Partnerships and Children

The stereotyped view of successful women who have made it to the top of organizational structures, is that they are single, and very dedicated singles, one dimensionally committed to their career. This was not the picture that emerged in the research undertaken here. There were certainly highly successful, single women who were often 'opinion-leaders' in their respective societies, but there were also married women with families who were at the top of their profession. From the results of this research, the idea of an entirely single-minded career woman, typical of the 'corporate profile' of the 1990s, dedicated to the organization, and with little thought of other aspects of life is certainly not borne out by the women interviewed here. The research was undertaken in Hong Kong and Singapore in 2001 and involved interviews with women in senior positions in academic, corporate, political and cultural life in both global cities. The women interviewed in Hong Kong and Singapore were certainly highly focused on their career, but not to the exclusion of other aspects of life, and most were interested in quality of life as well as quality of career. Both single and married women interviewed had given thought to how to accommodate careers, partners (and partner's careers) and relationships. There were of course personal reasons for this but there were also institutional factors which have been outlined elsewhere (see Brooks, 2001; Brooks and Mackinnon, 2001; Ramsay, 2001) which have produced this response. High achieving women are frequently making decisions where issues of intimacy and family life are seen as important (if not more important) than career decisions.

The issue of being single in these societies is the subject of both cultural and political pressure. Apart from family pressure oriented towards marriage and procreation there are also political pressures. It is probably fair to say that cultural pressures may be the predominant ones in Hong Kong while political pressures are more clearly defined in Singapore. The government of Singapore has done much to keep the preoccupation of Singaporean women on success within the context of the family through a range of measures designed to emphasize family values. The influx of migrant domestic labour encouraging men to play a full role in parenting, providing incentives in the form of couple matching agencies to encourage marriage, the introduction of a range of incentives to encourage larger families, through disadvantaging unmarried mothers by refusing them public housing and by encouraging the growth of 'family friendly firms'. As Purushotam states, given these advantages 'there is little sign of gender based discontent within the dominant texts of middle class modernity. The perception is that women have advanced and will continue to do so' (Purushotam, 1998, p.42).

Some of the single professional women interviewed who are in their late thirties and early forties were quite reconciled to singlehood and while not ruling out a partnership did not think that a partnership and particularly a family could fit into their career. A Senior Academic Administrator in Singapore, who was single, indicated that she had not deliberately avoided marriage and that she was fully aware that a family and children would demand more of her attention. She felt reconciled with her position as a single person, while accepting that she could have got a great deal out of marriage, and family life. On the question of whether she could see marriage fitting into her career, she said: 'I think … the career is hampering my opportunities, but I don't consciously seek to change that, because I do enjoy my work, and I don't see why I have to change it, in order to get married.' A Senior Research Fellow indicated that she had time to do what she wanted as she was not tied down by family considerations. At 48, she felt it was too late for her to talk about marriage but she did not rule out moving and starting a career elsewhere if she met a foreigner and decided to get married.

A Senior Vice-President of a company in Singapore reflected on the fact that at 40, she was coming under family pressure as regards marriage, and highlighted some of the difficulties confronting highly successful career women in Singapore:

> When I was younger there were a lot of people who wanted to date me, and I felt stressed going out for a date, because you've got this job to do. So I have actually turned down a lot of 'appointments'. As you go higher and higher on the corporate ladder, you are faced with a different set of problems, because then you are at a certain level, and I think I would prefer to go for somebody equal or even slightly under, I don't mind. But then you find that people are not there any more. The group of people who are at the senior management level, who are still single are relatively few. So there's a different sort of problem as you go up the corporate ladder.

When asked about the global corporate ladder and the fact that there are not only Singaporean executives out there, her response was that she was not sure whether she was ready to go out with people of different countries or races. She also felt that she would never get involved with a business colleague or customer. She felt that it would be easier to fit marriage into a career as opposed to a family as she indicated: 'I think that would be a challenge because given my current work hours and frequent travelling assignments, I think that would probably be a burden eventually. So this is the reason why marriage has never been my first priority.' In Hong Kong, a political 'opinion-leader' while single, was in a committed relationship and was learning from past experiences. With a profile of a well known 'opinion-leader' and spokesperson on democracy in Hong Kong society and a successful corporate and political background, she indicated quite candidly that she felt that where she had gone wrong was in her personal life. Age, which seem to preoccupy so many successful women in Singapore, was not really significant for this woman (or in fact for most women interviewed in Hong Kong), for her the emphasis was the issue of maturity. She had been married previously for a short time and attributed it to her immaturity. She felt that she could make up for things she had not done well before.

The stereotype of the successful, childless, single woman was certainly not one that characterized most of the professional women in this research. However the issue of children, and the responsibilities of childcare and family was a very big issue for many women. A Dean at the University of Hong Kong said that she had been able to advance quickly because she was childless, and she thought that makes it easier for a woman. She had wanted to have children but had found it did not fit into her career as it had developed. She explained that if she had had a child she would have given this priority and: '... it makes it impossible for a working mother to move on. You can imagine I would not have more than 10 books and hundreds of articles.' Similarly a Managing Director in Hong Kong also said she would give priority to marriage if it meant having children, and she also indicated that she would be prepared to take care of the children herself. The political 'opinion-leader' had a rather different attitude to motherhood:

> I never felt that motherhood was my dominant challenge in this life. I may or may not have children. I'm 46 years old, I have a committed relationship, but you know, life might pass me by on this experience. I'm happy with that. Also, my partner is very open minded, and we can adopt. So, I think, it's not the end of the world. I certainly don't feel that, even if I'm not going to have my own children, I don't feel that's a lesser life for me.

A Managing Director in Hong Kong saw a committed partnership as strengthening her career. She was co-habiting with a partner she had been with for seven months and saw no urgent need to get married, and as she indicated the way they were living was really no different from married life at all. She felt that a partnership gave psychological stability particularly when: '... you have a partner that you can basically communicate with emotionally. I think it really helps my career in some ways.' She had previously parted from a long term partner when their interests diverged and felt a spiritual as well as emotional affinity with her current partner:

> ... now with my current partner, we are very much in sync and we do everything together, even in our spiritual as well as cultural interests. To me, spirituality is very important ... for personal growth. And we both believe in spiritual enlightenment in terms of not particularly belonging to a religious group, we are Buddhist, but by our nature, basically we tend to spend our spare time doing charity works. That's what we feel will give us happiness and fulfillment. We are not fanatics, we do not go to the temples to pray, we live by example, that's what we do ... We don't believe in prayer, we believe in participation and behaving like a Buddhist in normal living conditions.

Marriage and Family Impacting on Career

On the question of marriage and family impacting on career, responses highlighted the compromises women continually make in attempting to achieve a balance between career and family. Several women had compromised on their careers because of their determination to maintain family issues as central in their lives. *The New York Times* cited Joan Williams, Director of the Program on Worklife Law at American University writing in the *Harvard Women's Law Journal* as stating that many women never get near the 'glass ceiling' because they are stopped long before by 'the maternal wall'. A Senior Educational Administrator for the legal profession in Hong Kong faced the same dilemma and conflict of interest between family and career, she indicated that she was not totally focused because she was always conscious of the fact that her son is quite young and needs assistance. For these reasons she compromised on how much time she was prepared to give her career:

> ... unlike a lot of barristers, I'm not prepared to work all night on a case. I won't stay that late, which probably has not helped my career development either, as a barrister ... Well not so much career development, but my practice I should say. Because you don't really develop your career, you just increase your practice. Which means earning more money, of course. So, yes, it has had an impact.

A Senior Lecturer in Law at the University of Hong Kong also confronted the issue of time shared between career and family and had made similar decisions about how she wanted to distribute her time: 'One of the reasons I wouldn't ever want to be head of department, or associate dean, if I could avoid it, is because I'd like to have a certain amount of time with my son. We only have one child and he's growing up fast and I don't want to waste those years. I do feel strongly about that.'

A Deputy Head of Department at a university in Singapore felt that family issues had had quite a significant impact on her career opportunities. There is a pattern within Singapore of academics being educated abroad at the government's expense and then returning to become academics within universities in Singapore. Those educated overseas, particularly in the US have the edge over those educated in Singapore. This academic woman had been faced with this decision about whether to undertake her doctorate overseas or locally, when her children were young. She felt she could not leave them behind for 4 to 5 years, so she opted to undertake her PhD locally. When it was pointed out that this could be beneficial in terms of familiarity with the Singapore system ... she said that it depended on the values of the organization, and she felt that (name of university) had a tradition of looking outwards and that an American education gives better value.

An Associate Professor at a university in Singapore, and a spokesperson on gender and issues of citizenship framed her response in terms of an understanding of gender ideology and politics:

> I am married to someone who very much agrees with my politics when it comes to gender. But I recognize, as he does, that if you are living within a patriarchal state, there are limitations as to how much you can push it. At the same time when I took maternity leave, for example, he didn't have the alternative of paternity leave. Very often when he made a stance about spending more time with the family, he would be asked you know ... where's your wife ... or that kind of question. So, for a while actually, he quite willingly would discuss the matter, and he quite willingly agreed to take a position for which his due rewards have not come to him. So, for about three years, he basically did not have a promotion nor increments. So we have worked within these limitations, but despite that, I would say that, a lot more of the home front falls into my responsibility. So there

are definitely gender imbalances. But I'm feminist enough to recognize that while the personal is political, he can only do so much to change things at a personal level.

It is clear that finding symmetry in terms of family and career is difficult to achieve for most women. Balancing marriage and career provided a profile of success for a Chair Professor in Medicine in Hong Kong, with three children and at the very top of her profession, as well as having a second career in the political realm, she had always worked more than 10 hours every day, she explained how the balance was achieved:

> Now of course you have three things, career, family and social life. What is sacrificed in this process is the social life. I didn't go out at night for dinner unless it was absolutely necessary, and didn't go out socially at weekends unless it was absolutely necessary, when the children were young. Weekends we do things with the children, take them swimming, water skiing, teach them to cycle, horseback riding, doing things together.

Her day would start at 7am with the children taken to school about 7.30am. She would get to the office at around 8am, and then deal with patients, teaching, and supervising research assistants. She would get home around 6 or 7pm, then have a brief rest, talk with the children and check their homework, and after they were in bed at 9pm, then she started her own 'serious' reading. This Chair Professor indicated that it was probably her time management that contributed most to her successful balance between career and family life.

Another stereotype of the successful professional career woman is one that prioritizes career over their family and husband/partner's career. The profile of the successful woman that emerged from this research shows a much more open attitude to career and more consideration of issues of quality of life, as opposed to career alone. Even highly successful single women at the top of the career ladder were prepared to consider giving up their career to accommodate a partner or husband's career. This is a very different profile of the successful woman from that of the corporate woman of the 1980s and 1990s that has been traditionally portrayed. It could be the case that, as one senior academic woman commented, having reached a certain point in one's career, other issues such as quality of life count far more, or it could be that successful women are now wanting more from life than a successful career alone.

An Academic Administrator at the National University of Singapore said she would give up her job if she thought it would enhance the welfare of the whole family. She felt that, in particular, if the education of the children is not affected and the overall welfare of the entire family is enhanced, then she would have no hesitation in giving up her career. A Research Fellow in Singapore said if her husband decided to go to Stanford, then she would have little difficulty in accommodating this move. A Senior Vice-President of a corporation in Singapore, who is currently single, and who was very committed to 'growing' the company reflected on whether she would give up elements of her career for a husband/partner. She said it would depend on who the other party was and how demanding they were and ideally the answer is 'no', however she indicated that if she met someone with a different set of requests, and felt that at that point that she would be prepared to make a decision in favour of marriage instead of career, then her main concern would be to find a successful successor.

In Hong Kong, the political 'opinion-leader' was wrestling with some of the same issues and admitted she did not know whether she would give up her career to accommodate her partner's career.

> I don't know. It's sort of the learning that we're going through right now, in terms of what do you want to do, and what do you want to do, and how to synchronize. Because I've found somebody who is very precious to me, and I think this could be a long term relationship, I am prepared, probably for the first time in my life to say, okay let's look at this differently. So this is a huge learning experience.

A Managing Director in Hong Kong, also unmarried and in a committed relationship, gave a similar reply saying that, 'Yes', she would give up her career to accommodate her partner's career if she felt it was necessary. A Senior Lecturer in Law at the University of Hong Kong indicated that while she would not give up her career in the sense that she would never give up working to accommodate her husband, she would consider making adjustments in her career if he was offered some fantastic position in the US and wanted to move. A Professor at the University of Hong Kong offered the same reflective position held by many of the women interviewed:

> Well, I think if you'd asked me that ten years ago, you would have got a very different response to now. Because I perceive myself as having reached a plateau in my career, partly through my own choice, and not aggressively moving forward, I suppose if somebody came along, and I was serious about him, that I was thinking of marriage, then depending on how I assessed the relative benefits of giving up elements of my career for marriage, I might decide to do that. Just on the grounds it was something different.

Not all women of course held this view, a Chair Professor in Medicine in Hong Kong said:

> No, I don't think so. I would go crazy. I can't stay at home. I'd probably end up doing other things too. So there was an understanding even before marriage that I would keep my career. I tried not working for one year, but it was disastrous. I was demanding, grumpy, I wanted evenings together, I wanted to go out on weekends, and of course he was busy and I said – it doesn't work.

A Senior Programme Director in Hong Kong felt that she had actually already given up her career to accommodate her husband even though she still in fact had a career.

> Well, I feel I have, and interestingly I am so lucky. I am very unique in Hong Kong, because the dynamic of Hong Kong life is usually the husband comes here and the wife trails after. But the wife is generally a very accomplished person in her own right, but ends up languishing in a beautiful home out in Stanley with an enormous expense account, and

is miserable. So I actually count myself lucky, even though I know I've given up an awful lot. I count myself as lucky because I have got a career of sorts, and I know that I am on the verge of making big changes. And I know that I've contributed to this society, which is important to me. I've also contributed to my own personal and professional realm. I've kept myself going here and so many other people. So whilst I believe … I've limited my career potential to accommodate my husband's career … I haven't given up my career in that sense.

'Filial Piety', Familial Obligations and Responsibilities

In both Hong Kong and Singapore the issue of 'filial piety' or the obligations of children to their families of origin remains a strong one for many Chinese families within these diasporic communities. In Singapore there is a pattern of children who remain single continuing to live with some form of the extended family, that is, continuing to live at home with their parents or mother and siblings. Thus in such cases familial bonds and obligations are very strong and were reflected in the comments made by a number of the contributors. A Senior Academic Administrator in Singapore, and one of the few women to really make it to the top academically in Singapore indicates that the conception of the normal family tends to focus on husband and children but she pointed out that there was often mother and siblings. She explained that her parents were divorced and she, as a single woman, lives with her mother and handicapped sister. She indicated that spending time with her mother and sister was very important; she also had no support services in the home. She commented as follows:

> … our conception of a normal family as husband, wife and children, very often leads us to forget that people who are not married also have family life. … I think we should not forget that the conception of the normal family can be quite as detrimental to a certain sector of women, as the view that is held of married women having difficulties … We often think of married women with children as the ones with problems, juggling work and family life, and a lot of our work tends to address that. But at the same time there are single women who also have families. I have a handicapped sister for example … I do have to care for her as well.

Several women interviewed felt that they were caught in the 'sandwich' generation. As a Chair-Professor in Medicine in Hong Kong commented:

> We look after our children and then because the lifespan is much longer you deal with elderly parents. And then there is always the problem of should you put them in a home, or can you still take care of them at home. Yes, probably you would have to put them in a home, and it's not only dealing with your parents, but your husband's parents.

While these issues are not peculiar to Chinese diasporic communities, two factors throw them into relief. The first is the clear obligation to support family members expressed in the notion of filial piety and secondly the lack of a social service infrastructure capable of dealing with these issues.

Spousal Attitude to Career, Parenting and Household

An interesting and significant dimension for the research was the issue of spousal attitudes to career, care giving/parenting, and household. In every case the partner/ spouse showed a very highly supportive attitude to career, in fact in many cases the spouse was said to aspire to more for the woman concerned. An Academic Administrator at a university in Singapore said that her husband was the single most important factor that contributed to her career development:

> He was the one that actually asked me to go and do a PhD. He said, you are an intellectual, and why don't you go further, because I know you won't be happy with a nine to five job … So he actually asked me to and pursue my dreams. So then I went ahead and pursued a PhD, and he followed suit and did his own PhD. So my husband is the most single important influence, he asked me to achieve the highest I could.

Also in Singapore, an Associate Professor's experience had been a similar one, she found her husband extremely supportive: 'In fact the times when I have said, no, I don't want to go for this conference, because my son is sitting an exam, it is he and my son who actually turn around and say you shouldn't be doing that, you should go, this is good for you.' A Senior Lecturer in Law at the University of Hong Kong said that her husband also encouraged her to go for more in career terms.

In some cases, shared career interests acted in a mutually supportive way between partners. A Dean at the University of Hong Kong felt fortunate that her husband is also an academic and head of department, and was also doing a lot of research:

> … so we basically carry our work home and after dinner we do some talking and then go back to our work. And we share a lot of work, and we know each other's work, so his position has been supportive. The reason I started working with chronic patients and cancer patients, and why I started to move out of community work, is because as time goes by we have nothing really to share. So he's working in oncology and I'm in community activism environmental protection. So after my PhD, I felt I'm free to do whatever I like, and after I chose to focus on two groups who are suffering in silence and in pain. One group of them are children in poverty, children and women in welfare. And the second group is chronic patients. So on the chronic patient side he helped a lot. He helped me identify the groups and make the contacts. Then he actually contributed, he participated in the work with chronic patients, and now we have formed an alliance with patient mental health groups. So there's a lot we share now.

Similarly a Managing Director in Hong Kong found her partner supported her in the social aspect of her work: 'In my business we have to entertain a lot and I like to entertain at home. Because I feel that creates a certain amount of intimacy, as well as breaking down barriers. And my partner has been extremely supportive of that.' Striking a balance between relationship and work time even with a supportive partner was something to be negotiated for the political 'opinion-leader' in Hong Kong: 'He's hugely supportive, but also ambivalent. In order to be successful I need to spend a lot of time doing it and that's time away from the relationship. So I'm more conscious of having to strike this balance. And I think I'm learning how to say 'No', because he's more important.'

Careers, while often different, did not detract from spouses being supportive. A Senior Educational Administrator for the legal profession in Hong Kong, when she told her husband, a career Civil Servant about her new position, found his response supportive and 'relieved':

> Delighted. He said at last you've got a proper job (laughs) ... charming! He's been very good. He's been very supportive in my career as a barrister, because it's been a lot of ups and downs. And you don't often get a lot of money, and sometimes you get a lot of money and sometimes you get a lot of money all at once. But you do spend your life chasing solicitors to pay you. It's not sort of guaranteed, so a salary every month will be a very pleasant change.

A Senior Programme Director at the University of Hong Kong found having different carriers did not pose too many problems as she commented:

> (Name of husband) is fantastic, in that respect. I've always earned more money than him. There's never been an issue. He's pissed me off by joking in company. 'Oh I don't know what my wife does but she's got the best job in Hong Kong, but I have no idea what she does', as in almost a put down. Whereas he's a lawyer, and you know what he does, everyone knows what he does. I've tackled him on that, and he agrees that it's not appropriate. But in every other sense, he has no issues with me being a working mother. He can't imagine it any other way. And, let's face it, it makes life a hell of a lot easier. And he's acknowledged that recently. He has not one other colleague in his law firm whose wife works or works to an equal level.

A Chair-Professor in Medicine in Hong Kong said that while her husband was in a very different career, in business, he was very relaxed and there was no competition, no comparison. When asked if he liked the fact that she was so successful, she responded as follows: 'I think he's not overjoyed about it, but he thinks, if you're doing something well you deserve to be successful ... his success is making money, I don't make much compared to him.' When it was pointed out that she had more status, she agreed but pointed out that in Hong Kong, it didn't matter, because money is also status.

As regards spousal attitudes to parenting and household, an Associate Professor in Singapore framed the debate in terms of gender equality and articulated what many of the women interviewed also felt.

> I aspire for him to have a completely equal role, but the aspirations have fallen short, and I recognize it and so does he. So there are constant negotiations. Sometimes it's because I myself slip into a pattern, like I was astounded when I look back, how when the baby first arrived, I had to consciously recognize that I was doing almost all of the caregiving work. And when I came to recognize it, we then began to negotiate how we could work on this and as I said he gave up his increment, his promotion for a while. As regards the parenting role, he has really done a lot of mothering and my child is very comfortable with him, and has an open relationship with him. It is true to say in some ways I've been there more for

him, because like the first day of school, it is I who would take the day off and take him. When he's sick, the sick child rule being such, you know, that I can take off to look after him much more easily than he can ... But in other respects, the normal day-to-day routine, he has played a crucial role.

A Deputy Head of Department at a university in Singapore also felt that her husband was good in a parenting role:

Well my husband does a fair bit of childcare. When the children were younger, because he had his own business he had a little more flexibility ... so he used to take them for their regular routine check-ups, or if they are not well he will take them to the doctors. Right now he helps them with some of their school work ... House-wise, I think he helps when he thinks I'm tired, but other than that he would help with the cooking during the weekend.

A Research Fellow in Singapore said that her husband said he would like to play 'Mr Mum' except that he is one of these scholars who cannot really afford to break his bond: 'So, is it equal? It is hard to say equal ... different.' An Academic Administrator in Singapore indicated that her husband was very positive and would play his part with parenting, but there had been no necessity for him to do so because they had always had domestic help. She indicated that his approach was very open: 'He was educated in New Zealand, and he's very western and keen, you know, equality. He's not the typical Asian male chauvinist, he's very different.'

In Singapore and Hong Kong the fact that most people had maids obviated to a large extent the need to share household tasks, and reduced some of the potential conflict within the parenting obligations. Despite this, problems did surface around taking responsibility. A Senior Programme Director in Hong Kong had two maids; yet felt that participation by her husband was a strong statement about equity.

A very contentious issue in my house, because in (name of husband)'s family, his father played no role whatsoever. (Name of husband) had no real training and I have had to really drag him into doing childcare/parenting role. He's been a willing participant but he hasn't actually seen the way in which I think he ought to be involved. So I'm very demanding in this respect.

A Senior Lecturer in Law at the University of Hong Kong was also very clear about her expectations of her husband's participation as regards both parenting and household responsibilities: 'I expect 50/50, I don't always get it, but I expect 50/50, I'm very vocal about that.' As regards caregiving, she spelt out the difference in attitude towards career vs. parenting:

It's very important to him and he does want to be an active father. He is, I think, a little more focused on his career than I am, so sometimes it gets sacrificed a bit more than it does for me. I mean he's more likely, for example, to accept an invitation to go to one more conference, even though he's already been away for a week. And I sometimes make it clear that I think he's going away too much. Whereas I'm more likely to say, I could go to that conference, but I've already been away, and I don't want another week away from my son. So I would think he's a little more focused on rising up than I am. Its more important to him than it is to me. And so that sometimes causes tensions, because it means that I wind up doing a little bit more of the childcare. But it's not a huge issue. Probably one of the reasons it's not a huge issue is because we do have domestic help. So I can walk in the door and I don't have to worry about making dinner. I don't have to worry about cleaning up. I can spend my time focused on my son. And I quite enjoy doing that. If I also had to negotiate the cleaning and all that other stuff with him, there might be more tension.

It is quite clear that the role of maids in Hong Kong and Singapore is a crucial one in facilitating an environment where dual career partnerships at the highest level, can survive and thrive. It is clear that professional women would be faced with considerably more pressures without maids. Where there was active participation by partner/husband it was regarded as having a novelty value and something of a trial by the women concerned. A Dean at the University of Hong Kong explained her husband's enthusiasm for housework in terms which parallel the gender division within an operating theatre: 'Now we have a part-time cleaner. When I was writing my doctorate, and all that part for my career, there was no such support. We were doing most of this ourselves. My husband is very active in housework. So I am always saying that in the kitchen, he is like a surgeon and I was like a nurse ... "Hand me the plate. Give me the fork."' A Chair Professor of Medicine in Hong Kong said she felt that parenting and household responsibilities should be split. As she noted: '... I expect that, but on the other hand I'd rather do the cooking, he likes to cook but he makes such a mess I spend more time cleaning the house. So it's not so much what I expect, it's what can be done more efficiently.'

In almost every case, for both single and married women, for those with children and those with other familial responsibilities, in Hong Kong and Singapore, all relied on support services in the home in the form of part-time or live-in maids. An Academic Administrator at the National University of Singapore chose domestic support in the form of a maid over institutional childcare for the following reasons: 'There are other conveniences and advantages that are attached to having a domestic maid at home. Because she also does the housework and cooking, whereas if I was to put my child in the childcare and not have a domestic maid, I would still have to do the household chores.' On the question of support structures, a Director of a Research Unit in Singapore said she relied on grandparents for the childcare, and a maid for household chores. An Associate Professor at a university in Singapore admitted: 'I have a full-time domestic maid and I must say there is no way I could cope without that arrangement. And there's no way my husband would be able to cope without that arrangement either. No way with respect to how we still insist on certain ways of organizing career and family work that is.'

In Hong Kong, among the women interviewed, all had support in the form of maids and in some cases this was extended. A Senior Programme Director at the University of Hong Kong felt the absence from her children on a daily basis so much that she had attempted to frame a familial structure:

I have two helpers. I feel very keenly, as I said before, my absence from my family. So I have two children, and I have two helpers ... Well I have one who is very well educated, they're both Filipinas. They are both very distinct, in their qualifications I guess. One was brought up in an American home, has linguistic skills as capable as yours and mine. She's me, she's mum, so she's the nanny. And her sister-in-law is the housekeeper. And having said that, I have been so enormously lucky, they've been with me forever ... We have a very stable household.

A Senior Lecturer in Law in the University of Hong Kong also had a live-in helper also from the Philippines who had been with them for seven years and who she described as 'Wonderful'. The helper looked after the son, cleaned the house, did the laundry and most of the shopping. Another long term live-in situation existed for a Chair Professor in Medicine:

Yes a domestic helper, who serves as the housekeeper, she is a marvellous person and has worked for us for twenty years. She was my sister's domestic helper in the Philippines, and when my sister left for the United States she came to work for us. She was the nanny, she was the housekeeper, I trust her completely. She's very good at repairing things and doing carpentry work.

Maids are the norm in countries like Hong Kong and Singapore although still seen as a luxury in the West. But chauffeurs are also quite normal in Hong Kong, particularly for those in the upper echelons of government or the corporate world. A Senior Educational Administrator for the legal profession in Hong Kong said that she had a maid who did all household chores and acted as nanny: '... we did say when our present maid left, we'd get a couple, so that the husband could drive us, because with the drink-driving laws, neither of us could afford to.' A Managing Director of an aviation company in Hong Kong said: 'I have a maid and also a chauffeur.'

Conclusion

This chapter has provided a snapshot of some of the issues around intimacy, work and family life confronting professional women in Singapore and Hong Kong. The professional women interviewed in this research certainly did not conform to the stereotype of the successful, ambitious woman, single-mindedly focused on career. Intimacy figured largely in their views of their careers and they were reflective and empathetic, constantly negotiating personal and social spaces in relation to their career. Many had reached the point where striving for the top position, while still attractive, had to be set against quality of life, and many were less prepared to make too many sacrifices for career. The findings show that women in the academic and corporate world were making more decisions in favour of intimacy and relationships, quality of life, even spirituality, and no longer wanted or desired a top position if the sacrifices, as they saw them, were too great, factors such as partners and spouses were significant in final decision making. Issues common to all research of this type, such as ongoing negotiations around parenting and taking responsibility within the household, remained significant for many women, particularly in Hong Kong, although in all cases the existence of support structures in the home in the form of maids alleviated many of the immediate tensions.

Chapter 6

The New Economy, Professional Women and Social Change

This chapter examines three aspects of the debate around the global impact of the new economy, gender and social change. Firstly it focuses on the new economy and the growing differentiation of gendered labour in global cities. Secondly it considers a number of global issues and how these impact on professional women in global cities, and finally it looks at how these issues shape the debate around gender, social and organizational change in the specific context of Hong Kong and Singapore. The issue of social change has been a significant theme throughout this book, and many of the issues raised in this chapter reflect on economic, political and social changes taking place in Hong Kong and Singapore. Organizational change frequently follows legislative and policy changes, and the direction of such debates is highly significant for the future growth of Hong Kong and Singapore and the positioning of women in these debates.

The New Economy, Global Cities and the Feminization of Labour

The new economy has produced social divisions that are accentuated in global cities, which finds the greatest accumulation of highly paid workers positioned alongside low paid workers. The position of women in the labour force highlights this duality. A significant minority of women have reached the highest paid sectors (if not the very top jobs), however women are still overwhelmingly represented in low paid areas of work. As Perrons (2004, p.222) notes: 'These two phenomena are organically related as the continuing unequal division of labour means that the increase in the number of high paid women workers leads to an increase in the demand for marketed personal services and care.'

Perhaps the most dramatic impact of the new economy has been the feminization of labour at every level of the economy. The labour force participation rate (LFPR) of women has been increasing globally. The LFPR measures the proportion of the population who are in the labour force, expressed as a ratio of the population as a whole, for the same age category. The increase in female participation rates should not be equated with gender equality and barriers remain at every level for women. An interesting situation is developing where gender equality policies are operating nationally and globally and increasing numbers of women are entering the workforce, but the terms and conditions of their employment are increasingly insecure (Perrons, 2004; Standing, 2002).

Regardless of these changes women remain significantly under-represented in management and leadership positions. Figures for the European Union (EU) show that only 21 percent of the workforce have a woman in a managerial position compared with 63 percent who have a male manager. In addition women managers are far more likely to be supervising other women, and less than 10 percent of men have a woman manager (Perrons, 2004, p.85; Fagan and Burchell, 2002). Despite the limitations and the overall increase in the total burden of responsibilities, studies show that the overall impact of paid employment is positive for women which increases their empowerment, bargaining power and self-esteem.

The new economy has fundamentally changed the relationship between work and family and has for many professional women redefined their lives. Indeed for many professional women the benefits of a 'serviced' home life carries more attraction than domestic work and childcare (Reeves, 2001). The impact of the new economy on workers is that they are highly paid but 'time starved' (Perrons, 2004) and this leads them to demand a range of services that are either supplied by the employer or catered for by low paid female migrant workers.

Changes resulting from the economic restructuring caused by the new economy have led to a widening of the earnings gap between those at the top and those at the bottom for both men and women. However the multiplicity of social divisions emerging shows an intersecting pattern of skills, gender and ethnicity. The complexity of social divisions is no longer tied to ethnicity as Perrons (2004, p.221) notes: 'There are some highly paid female ethnic minority IT and finance workers, and ethnic majority workers living on or below the minimum wage, thus these divisions take multiple forms.'

The pattern of professional and managerial work requires very long hours of work and employers and employees have adjusted to these demands. Employees have opted out of legislative directives on working time, and employers are increasingly providing a range of on-site services for their employees including crèche, restaurants, gym, physiotherapist, dentist and nurse. The interesting element of highly paid workers at this level is that whereas firms have equal opportunities and family friendly policies, employees see it as a disadvantage to their careers to be taking advantage of them. Other services provided by employers include dry cleaning services, grocery shopping services, cookery classes, etc.

Many other professional women employ a range of domestic service support including domestic cleaners, childcare workers and nannies. In Asia and in many other parts of the world live-in maids are commonplace for both total domestic services and childcare and two maids per household is not uncommon. These domestic service patterns are also characterized by gender, class and ethnicity as Perrons (2004, p.105) outlines:

> Care chains are typically racialized as Caucasian workers are generally paid more than Asians and Asians more than those of African descent. In Rome, the Filipinos are

paid more than people from Cape Verde (Tacoli, 1999) and in Canada, Filipinos are 'housekeepers' and have to combine housework with childcare, even though the Filipino may be a university graduate and the European a qualified nursery nurse but with fewer years of education (Pratt, 1999).

In many cases migrant domestic female labour are themselves employing much lower paid workers to look after their own families in their country of origin. Arlie Hochschild (2000) describes the situation of 'Vicky Diaz', a college educated Filipino and who is currently employed in Los Angeles earning 400 US dollars a week working as a nanny in a wealthy American family. She pays a live-in worker in the Philippines 40 dollars a week to look after her family of five. In the last nine years she has only spent three months with her family. She is trying to legalize her position to reunify her family in the US.

The global city is the locus of the most highly paid and lowest paid workers. Highly paid professional women are earning sufficient income to enable them to afford domestic live-in help and childcare. Women from a wide range of backgrounds can progress within an organization but most do not. A range of obstacles still confront women in the professions including prejudice and discrimination operating through male power structures which continue to exclude and marginalize women (McDowell, 1997). Female workers in Hong Kong and Singapore have higher occupational status then their counterparts in other Asian countries and both Hong Kong and Singapore have a relatively large proportion of women in managerial and professional positions (Thang and Yu, 2004).

The New Economy, Professional Women and Social Change

The 'new economy' debate has already been identified as an important factor in advancing opportunities for professional women while reinforcing new patterns of inequality based on ethnicity and gender. It has also been noted that both the Singapore and Hong Kong governments have been instrumental in directing social policy debates with the aim of advancing technological change and the growth of the global knowledge economy. At the same time the Singapore government, in particular, is promoting strong neo-natalist policies, as well as giving greater emphasis to promoting family values. As has been shown, even in a country such as Hong Kong that has the highest proportion of professional women in Asia, the mass media continues to stigmatize women in professional occupations who do not fall into the traditional home maker image. An Academic Administrator at the National University of Singapore stated that the government in Singapore was trying to encourage both family values and women as income earners, and is realizing the need to seriously explore flexi-hours. She indicated that with most families consisting of dual income earners, there was a recognition that children were now being brought up by maids and that this is 'unhealthy'. She observed: 'So they are wanting to allow more flexible hours for the mother to be able to stay home, and work from home, because of the fear of bringing up a whole new generation of children under foreign maids, and suffering a decline in values.' A Deputy Head of Department was more concerned about the implications of the neo-natalist policy for women: 'You find that the government is saying that we are encouraging women to have more babies. Now whether that would have implications on people in terms of ability, in terms of time, and in terms of talent, to actually be in a very senior management post, it is difficult to say.' I asked her whether this policy worried her, she responded as follows:

> Yes, in terms of women in general ... I think society as a whole is expecting too much of women ... And I don't think its because the husbands are not giving the support, its just that generally society as a whole is putting a lot of pressure on people to perform. And we've got to do everything. I think its up to the individual to decide what they are going to be happy with.

A Director of a Research Unit at a university in Singapore said that equality in the domestic sphere was a necessary precursor to greater equality in the workplace. She noted that women are often in deputy positions, but there are few women leaders right at the top in the university. She maintained that change would be slow given the gender imbalance in academia to start with.

So how are corporate women faring relative to their academic counterparts and to their counterparts in other countries? In addition, do the same opportunities exist for women in local companies, as compared with the appointment of expatriate or local women to multi-national companies? I asked a Senior Vice-President in Singapore whether she noticed any differences in terms of opportunities for women. She responded as follows:

> I think in Singapore ... I do not feel much discrimination against women in senior positions, whether in private or governmental organization ... there are quite a few women up there, though comparing with men, it is still relatively fewer than men. I think in other countries, you will find far fewer women in senior positions, for example Taiwan. I dealt with Taiwan relatively frequently and I do not remember seeing a lot of female executives, unless they are the daughter of the founder. Some countries, in addition, like Japan and Korea, are similar. In American multinationals, you can find some women in CEO positions, but again relatively few, not a high percentage. But do they have resistance to going up the corporate ladder ... I would not like to say at all, but in the IT industry you can see quite a few successful women over there, but I'm not sure about finance, and other organizations, whether they have the same opportunities.

In Hong Kong the pace of economic change has been accelerated by social and political changes. Perhaps the most dramatic changes have occurred in Hong Kong as a result of the return of the Hong Kong to China and its removal from colonial status. A Dean at the University of Hong Kong, while sympathetic to the interests of the Chinese, felt that the impact of the 'handover' in 1997 was not altogether beneficial:

The social changes that have happened in the past few years, since the return to China, has been moving to a more conservative, traditional patriarchy. Respect for elders, business interests, far more than respect for individual rights, whether gender, sex or age. So I would think women's status has slipped in these few years, despite the increasing number of women in high positions.

I asked her what she thought were the reasons for the shift. She responded as follows:

Public sentiment as a result of unemployment. Women, the displaced manufacturing women workers, go into the service sector. But the service sector extension has sort of stopped. Further displaced workers have no jobs and the husbands have no jobs as well, and when the women have to go out to find work, the men feel humiliated, and suspicious of her developing other relationships. There is an increasing amount of domestic violence. Also because of the opening up of China, more men go back to China for commercial reasons, with increasing numbers of divorces and unhappy marriages in Hong Kong. This all happened in the last 3-4 years. So I would say that with evidence of increasing numbers of domestic violence, rapidly increasing divorce rates, lowering of income among working class people, both men and women, have all put women in a worse position.

These observations operate at both lower level and professional positions as is evidenced by the media reports of the economic 'backlash' against women.

Political and Legislative Change

The Sex Discrimination Ordinance and the Equal Opportunities Commission (EOC) were identified by a Senior Lecturer in Law and also a Professor at the University of Hong Kong as significant aspects of social change in Hong Kong and enormous achievements for women. As the Senior Lecturer in Law noted:

That happened in 1996, but the impact is only gradually being felt. But apart from that I can't think of any significant developments that have really opened up things for women. And I think there's still a long way to go. And one of the things that really upsets me is that the EOC's formal investigation of the government's system for allocating students to secondary schools found that the system discriminated against women ... Women still earn something like 80 percent of what men earn. So I think that gradually the legislation and EOC activities, will open more things up for women.

However, a Professor at the University of Hong Kong recognized that the existence of the legislation did not guarantee non-discriminatory practices for women, particularly 'grass-roots' women. As she noted:

I represent a particular segment and slice of Hong Kong women. I can't speak for grass-roots women. And of course, university women have as much right to an identity and a voice as any other group of women, but they're not representative of Hong Kong women ... If you were interviewing grass-roots organizations, women in grass-roots women's organizations, you'd be hearing very different things, very different priorities, and probably far more hands-on discriminatory experiences than university women have experienced. Because there are structures here [in the university] like equal pay, anyone working for the government, men and women on the same grade get the same money. So there isn't that constant fight over wages at the university for women that there would be say for women working in business or manufacturing industries.

Some of the women interviewed in this research had been directly involved in the social changes being experienced in Hong Kong and Singapore. A Senior Lecturer in Law at the University of Hong Kong had become involved with the development of the Bill of Rights Ordinance and anti-discrimination legislation, as well as with providing a forum for these, and other issues of academic freedom and sexual harassment through a range of international publications. She explained her involvement with the Bill of Rights and Equal Opportunities legislation in Hong Kong:

> In the Fall of 1989, it was a big opportunity for women's groups, because that's when the Hong Kong Government first proposed the Bill of Rights. Up until then the Hong Kong government kept saying that the people didn't need a bill of rights in Hong Kong because they were protected after '97 by the Basic Law, and there was enough human rights provision in the Basic Law. But then of course in the summer of '89, the Tiananmen Square massacre occurred. If you have read anything about it, you will know that something like 20 percent of the population of Hong Kong was out in the streets marching. And so in the Fall of '89, my first year of teaching, the government really wanted to do something to reassure people, and one of the things that they did was to propose the Bill of Rights. They circulated a draft Bill in the Fall of '89, right when I was teaching the Hong Kong legal system. I remember I was practically teaching the course out of the newspapers. For women it was a real door of opportunity because there were equality provisions in the Bill of Rights. They did, I think, a very good job of identifying equality as a human right. They did an excellent job of making people understand that human rights wasn't just free speech, freedom of association, freedom of movement, but that it also included a right of basic equality. And they really allied themselves very well, I think, with the human rights organizations. And so the entire year, the women's groups were working on this draft bill and making submissions to the Legislative Council. In fact, we couldn't really have much influence on what was in the Bill, because everybody knew that in the end the government was basically going to copy the ICCPR (International Covenant on Civil and Political Rights), and that was because the ICCPR was already mentioned in the Basic Law. So they [the government] felt if they kept the Bill of Rights Ordinance exactly, or almost exactly worded as the ICCPR it would be harder for China to repeal. The ICCPR is one of the most important international human rights conventions. When the UK and China agreed on the Joint Declaration, the UK negotiators persuaded China to agree that the ICCPR would continue to be enforced in Hong Kong after 1997. That was actually a very key agreement. Then they drafted the Bill of Rights Ordinance, which was enacted in the summer of 1991, and the courts started enforcing it in Hong Kong. This helped the courts to develop a whole jurisprudence regarding judicial review of legislation and executive action.

She pointed out that, in addition, the discussion around the Bill of Rights as to whether the Bill of Rights Laws were to be enforceable against private parties, which women's organizations were pushing for, resulted in the education of the Legislative Council (LegCo) members and in an agreement to consider introducing anti-discrimination legislation. I asked her whether the women's movement in Hong Kong was driven by Western women, or was it more representative of local women. She said she thought it was a mix although there were people who definitely wanted to call it a Western driven activity. She said they were known as the 'WWWs' of Hong Kong – the 'White Whinging Women' of Hong Kong. She thought it wasn't really expatriate driven and there were lots of local women's organizations that were involved. She felt that the Western women's participation was generally welcome by the women's movement, primarily because the business of government was largely conducted in English. Lobbying was still very much done in English. She felt English and Chinese speaking groups assisted one another and, further, that since transition the role of Western women has become a little less significant in the organizations, because you do not have to speak English to lobby the government.

She gave the following summary of the debate around the Sex Discrimination Ordinance and the significance of women 'opinion-leaders' in the process:

> I believe that the Sex Discrimination Ordinance might not have been enacted if it wasn't for the handover, because if it wasn't for the handover, we probably would not have got the Bill of Rights Ordinance ... So to me, the whole emphasis on human rights and building democracy made it easier for women to lobby. I was lucky because I was invited to help Anna Wu with her Equal Opportunities Bill in 1993. She was an appointed legislator, appointed by Chris Patten. When he came here, he made a few liberal appointments, such as Christine Loh and Anna Wu. Anna Wu's main focus was to get an anti-discrimination bill through, and so she came to the university for some assistance.

I asked her to elaborate on the role of Anna Wu and Christine Loh within the legislative process and within the Legislative Council:

> I think Anna Wu was a little better known, because she had done work with the Consumer Council already, and they were popular with the community. They were adventurous appointments, because both of these women would end up introducing Private Members Bills that directly challenged government policy. Chris Patten actually prevented Anna Wu's Human Rights Commission Bill from being considered by LegCo (Legislative Council). So he was the one that put her in, but in the end they were clashing. But I think he respected those women, and I think he realized that those views needed to come in. Some people might be a bit more cynical and say that the British Government was making trouble for China ... China wasn't happy about that. Between Christine Loh's Access to Information Bill and Anna's Wu's Equal Opportunities Bill (EOB) ... I mean they had major influences on government policy, because the government was forced to introduce compromise bills, to prevent these other bills being enacted.

She worked with women's organizations in Hong Kong to encourage support for Anna Wu's Equal Opportunities Bill. She indicated that a number of women's organizations preferred to support the Government's Bill (Sex Discrimination Ordinance), because they felt it was a sure thing and also because it just dealt with sex. As she indicated some of them weren't really sure that they wanted to support Anna's Bill, which also would have prohibited discrimination in regard to sexuality and certain other things that they weren't quite sure they wanted to support.

> They were very happy that she wanted to prevent discrimination on the ground of age. That's something that they really wanted to get through, and they couldn't persuade the Government to include ... I do think that it was in that period of time that the local women's organizations became more independent from the expatriate women ... because it was in that period of time that LegCo started dealing more in Chinese, and it was more natural for people to come in and give submissions in Chinese ... And even some legislators, who I think were more comfortable speaking in English, felt they could speak in Chinese.

Education and Academic Leadership

Education is clearly an area that offers women one of the main opportunities for social advancement, tertiary education in particular is an area where women have benefited most. A Professor at the University of Hong Kong charted the advances for women in education:

> Education became compulsory in 1978, which is not really very long ago. Which means that there is no significant illiteracy among women in Hong Kong, unless they were born in China. Women born in Hong Kong have the same literacy standards overall as men born in Hong Kong. And as has been noted, young women appeared to be outperforming young men in exams at school, and in entrance to university. Now presumably, as that process has been going on for a while, this means the opening up of tertiary education to women. I mean it's never been closed to women; it's just that they never managed to jump all the hurdles to get there. But nowadays that seems to have changed, say in the last ten years. I think the sheer mass of women coming through the education system at its top levels is inevitably going to have consequences. But I am not sure to what extent they are going to be consequences that are predicted and supported by the government, as a result of equal opportunities policy.

A Chair-Professor in Medicine in Hong Kong who had researched the data on women in education for a paper for the World Health Organization commented as follows: 'From the work we've seen in medical schools, it used to be 10-20 percent of the applicants or students were female, now its 50 percent and probably going higher. We see that also in finance, and in pure science. Women are not only better educated, but they are also going into fields which were in the past considered masculine domains.' She made the additional comment that women in Hong Kong had always been accepted into senior positions in government and business. I asked her whether the 'handover to China' had had any impact on these trends. She responded as follows:

No, it's always been that way. It's even more so than before. Business has to do with family, a lot of businesses in Hong Kong are still family business, so the daughter, if she is any good, runs the business. And I think even many of the senior people in big companies are women and that's because of ability really, more than connections. And in academia it goes up and down, we used to have a lot more female professors, but there are less now because less have applied. It's a hard life; it's a harder life than it used to be.

This Chair-Professor in Medicine in Hong Kong had had a very smooth path to the top of her career, and at the point of retiring, reflected on her success in academic and political life in Hong Kong. She had trained in Oxford, and had been very influenced by her father. She originally started off in neurology before moving to psychiatry. On arriving in Hong Kong there was no dedicated academic department, which was established in the 1970s. I have outlined elsewhere in this book, the dual track career of some of the professional women involved in the research. She combined an academic with a political career. The political career of this Chair-Professor was as prestigious as her academic career, with a series of government appointments, culminating in being asked to join the Cabinet of the last Governor of Hong Kong, and before that, being appointed to the Legislative Council. I asked her if she had sought out a political career, she responded as follows:

No, never, but I enjoy taking on challenges, and I think the political career came along because of my involvement in many of the social issues which were relevant to my area of work. For instance I was one of the first people in Hong Kong to write about child-abuse. At that time nobody even knew what child abuse was all about. And that study is still considered a classic as far as Hong Kong history of child-abuse is concerned. Also I was one of the first people to talk about autistic children in the Chinese, because before that, everybody thought that the Chinese race is exceptional, and there was no autism, and of course we found that to be the contrary. We focused on the family training of parents who have disturbed children and then the collaborative work with the schools with hyperactive children. So it was mainly those things that brought the appointments to the Government Advisory Board on Social Welfare. Then something which I enjoyed thoroughly being asked to be a member of the Government 'think-tank', and from there onto the Cabinet.

This Chair-Professor still sits on a number of important government advisory committees and has recently stepped down from being Chairperson of the Medical Council. She still sits on the Law Reform Commission, and when I asked her how she found her role on the Commission, she responded as follows: 'I think it's a very interesting role to pick up, because then one can sort of try to mould society, through legislative means. But then, not being a lawyer, I can always of course give the lay opinion, and how lay people perceive the problem, and how it should be legislated.' She was planning to retire at 60, which is the mandatory retirement age. I asked her about this as she has such a distinguished career, it seemed so early to consider not translating it into something for the future, as she is the consummate professional in so many aspects of life and Hong Kong society. Her response was typically pragmatic: 'Of course I could have asked for an extension, but I thought there's more to life than just an academic career. I would like to do other things, like learn art history, play golf, travel more, in a more relaxing way.' I asked her if she was interested in a diplomatic post. Her answer was firm:

> No. I have worked in government; I know what government is. I have worked in international organizations, like being a consultant for WHO [World Health Organization], and working on some World Bank projects, and for three years from '93-'96 I was President of the Royal Society. I know what the international community is all about and I don't want the hassle of working in that kind of organization anymore.

The Global Knowledge Economy

The growth of the knowledge economy and global trade were seen by both academic and corporate women as facilitating the advancement of women in the Hong Kong and Singapore economies. The knowledge economy and its implications was seen as a real engine of growth in Hong Kong by a Senior Programme Director at the University of Hong Kong as she noted:

> I'm very conscious of living in an economy where knowledge is paramount, and also where talent is limited, because what I've found here is a lot of capability, a lot of intellectual ability, but very few people who can actually see beyond the box … or otherwise think about bigger issues or why are we doing this … I find Hong Kong fantastic in that regard, and fabulous for women, because we all have access to it. And I think that's a wonderful reflection on this society.

Similarly a Managing Director saw the Hong Kong government as open to global trade and she saw both Hong Kong and China as encouraging women to move into leading positions.

In this regard a number of remarkable women 'opinion-leaders' were identified as making significant contributions to changing the face of Hong Kong. A Professor at the University of Hong Kong noted that before the 'handover' to China three remarkable women in particular set the scene: 'Emily Lau, Christine Loh and Anna Wu, were a very impressive trio of role models for young Hong Kong women.' A Managing Director in Hong Kong saw Anson Chan as opening up a lot of opportunities for women in higher positions, as she observed:

> In Hong Kong right now we have a lot of very high profile professional women … also in Hong Kong women basically have the same sort of remuneration as their male partners. So it's your capability, whether you can do the job, if you are capable then you will be paid appropriately. It's not only social changes in Hong Kong but also in China. When you look at China in government positions, a lot of leading positions are held by women.

Human Rights and Political Representation

A political opinion-leader and frequent spokesperson on political representation and freedom of speech in Hong Kong on CNN and BBC World Television, is Chief

Executive Officer of Civic Exchange, an independent policy think-tank in Hong Kong, a former politician, and senior executive in corporate life. As CEO of her own organization, I asked her to comment on the issue of women within the context of corporate and political life and to chart her rise to the top in political and corporate life. Her political involvement, and corporate success have always operated in tandem.

She joined the 'Hong Kong Observers' in the late 1970s and, as she indicates, it was the best respected armchair commentator in Hong Kong. She saw it as a prelude to political activities. At the same time she was working for a multi-national company called Philipp Brothers. She was sent to Beijing for six months: 'I was amongst the first group of business people to go into China. In fact I helped set up the first US representative office in Beijing. Now at the time, none of this seemed very important, but looking back, I think it had historical significance.' She elaborated on this point:

> Well in those days in China, and this is 1980, China had only started her modernization process, her so-called 'Open-door Policy', in 1978-79, so we really were the first batch of people to be living and working in China as non-Chinese … non-local business representatives … I learnt a lot about China. A lot of people in political life, later on said I didn't know anything about China, but that's not actually true … I've been going to China a lot longer than a lot of other people. I came back to Hong Kong to learn *Putonghua* (Mandarin), when *Putonghua* was not even fashionable. So I think I have an unusual background, to be amongst the first to go to China to do business. Amongst the first really of my generation of Hong Kong Chinese to actively learn *Putonghua*. I never thought I would actually go into politics as such. I wasn't sure that what we did in terms of public affairs commentary with the Hong Kong Observers was 'politics' as such. But what was interesting about 'The Observers' was that I was actually involved in quite an active way in shaping the discussion, the Sino-British discussion. Because we were so obviously a group of bright young things in Hong Kong that both the British and China governments were quite keen to have us on their side. And we did write publicly, and we did have a public platform. We did have ideas. And in 1983, the Hong Kong Observers were invited to go to Beijing to present a policy paper about the transfer of power. So we were kind of involved from Day 1.

She noted that there were other members of the Hong Kong Observers who became significant figures in formulating policy in Hong Kong. The Convenor of the Executive Council, C.Y. Leung, the former as well as the current head of the Equal Opportunities Commission and Former Legislator, Anna Wu. She remained with the multi-national company for 12 years and became Regional Managing Director and despite her involvement with the Hong Kong Observers saw herself as a corporate. It was not until 1992 when she was invited to become a member of the Legislative Council in Hong Kong that she really began to see herself as a politician. As indicated earlier she was invited by the Chief Secretary, Sir David Ford, in 1992, acting on behalf of the then new Governor of Hong Kong, Chris Patten to serve on the Legislative council in 1992. Both she and Anna Wu were picked from the Hong Kong Observers, as she commented: '… folks with a public record in democracy.'

In 1991, the first direct elections were held for 18 of the 60 seats in the Legislative Council. Petersen (1996, p.362) notes that the remaining seats were constituted as follows: 3 ex-officio seats (held by members of the Hong Kong government and therefore guaranteed government votes); 18 appointed members; and 21 members elected by functional constituencies. Petersen (1996, p.362, N83) also observes that:

> Traditionally, appointed members could be counted upon to vote with the government if urged to do so. But some appointed members have shown greater independence. For example, Anna Wu and Christine Loh, both Patten appointees during the 1991-95 term, introduced private members bills that directly challenged government's established policies. Loh was elected as one of the directly elected seats in the 1995 elections. Wu, a solicitor, chose not to stand for election in 1995.

Petersen (1996) details the involvement of Christine Loh within the Legislative Council particularly with the issue of the right of female inheritance to land in Hong Kong, and the issues that emerged around The New Territories Land (Exemption) Bill. Petersen (1996, p.344) outlines the background to this situation. She points out that 'even in the 1990s, the consultative system in the New Territories villages … systematically excluded women.' This included not allowing women to stand for election as Village Representatives. One of the most conservative bodies reinforcing traditional practices in the New Territories is the Heung Yee Kuk. Petersen (1996, p.344) describes this group as a traditional male-dominated body that wields enormous power in the New Territories because the (British) government in Hong Kong made it its 'statutory advisory body on New Territories matters'. Christine Loh stood out against the Heung Yee Kuk during her time as an appointed member of the Legislative Council. During the debate on The New Territories Land (Exemption) Bill, Loh 'announced that she would propose an amendment to the Bill, so as to exempt rural as well as urban land from the ban on female inheritance' (ibid., p.368). Petersen notes that the government did not oppose Loh's amendment even though it was aware of the response of the Heung Yee Kuk, as she observes, the government was probably relieved that a member of the Legislative Council had taken over responsibility for challenging the power of the group. Petersen (1996, pp.370-71) outlines the significance of Loh's intervention and the upheavals that followed:

> The amendment proposed by Loh did not require land-owners to leave their land to their female heirs, and any landowner who wished to leave his or her land only to male heirs would still be able to do so by simply making a will. Thus, the only effect of Loh's amendment was to give landowners the right to leave land to their female heirs. Nonetheless, the Heung Yee Kuk and conservatives in the New Territories strongly opposed the amendment and organized very emotional (and at times violent) protests against it, frequently making front-page news … However public opinion polls showed that the majority of the Hong Kong people supported Ms Loh's amendment and that her chances of winning a directly elected seat in the Legislative Council … had increased significantly as a result of the issue.

I asked this political opinion-leader about her political leadership qualities, as she was clearly someone who is unafraid, confident in her own views, and prepared to speak out on a range of issues. I wondered whether these qualities had developed during her corporate, or political experience. She responded as follows:

> The root of that does not come from political or business career. It comes from my family and values that have been there for a long time. I'm Catholic, I had a traditional Catholic upbringing, I went to a Catholic school. I have Judaeo-Christian values that were drummed into me subconsciously. I think those really are my foundations, my security. The basic message is do good, and speak out for those who cannot speak for themselves. I feel strongly about that.

She demonstrated these qualities and those of a key 'opinion-leader' in Hong Kong in the face of social change, during her period as elected representative in LegCo from 1995:

> In 1995 I won the election. We knew we were going to be kicked out in '97. Between '95 and '97, I felt there was a sense of urgency for me to do whatever I could in the areas that I know something and care about in terms of legislative reform. So between 1995 and 1997, I took some of the remaining work of Anna Wu on Equal Opportunities by amending the Sex Discrimination Ordinance, and the Disability Discrimination Ordinance. Then there was Article 30 of the Prevention of Bribery Ordinance. On a personal basis it was the most satisfying piece of law reform that I've ever done. I also created a completely new idea for a piece of law, called the Protection of the Harbour Ordinance which is still there today. I very much wanted to get those things out of the way; it was at the height of the Sino-British row. What I wanted to do was to bang on about Hong Kong's basic values and freedoms and our aspirations for democracy. But I also wanted to see whether it was possible to start a dialogue with China ... I have the greatest respect for China. And I do understand very often where they are coming from. So I wanted to see whether it was possible for people in the democratic camp to start a dialogue with China. It was very difficult and the dialogues were very painful. They wanted you to essentially, agree with them ... My colleagues in the democratic camp were highly critical of me even showing an interest, and taking steps to have a dialogue with Chinese officials. They saw that as a sell-out. So I got hugely criticized for undertaking that very mild step. Then we were kicked out of office in '97. At the time, we didn't know when there would have been elections. There was no way I was going to get my seat back ... So I sat it out for a year. I then worked for the Citizens Party which was actually a sort of new 'greenie type party'.

She continued her active leadership of the Citizens Party and within the Legislative Council (LegCo) until 2000, when she decided to step down. She turned her attention to how best to lobby for issues that concerned her most and she decided that operating outside LegCo would give her more flexibility. She felt that what Hong Kong needed was an independent non-profit think-tank and hence Civic Exchange was formed. She described its *raison d'etre* as follows:

> We are aiming for international think-tank quality work. This is not a political commentary body. We are here to do serious think-tank public policy. One thing I realized from my

political career, is that you can have the best ideas in the world, but if you don't know how to popularize it, to get it out to politicians, media, business and members of the public, then you may not actually be able to change anything.

I asked her what would she say defined her as a successful leader in corporate and political life. She thought that she was entrepreneurial, a risk-taker but within clearly defined parameters. As she commented: 'I don't think I was jumping into an abyss, I thought this is an interesting opportunity. I didn't know everything about the opportunity, but it looked interesting enough, and I felt that I could quite comfortably try it. But, I think the fearless side is really part of the personal foundation that comes from family and upbringing.'

Shaping the Debate around Gender and Civil Society

Many women interviewed in Singapore had also made a real contribution to social and organizational change. One contributor did bring a gender perspective to the equation and many in Singapore would see her as certainly a spokesperson on issues of gender, ethnicity and class in Singapore. An Associate Professor at a university in Singapore, described the most pressing concern in Singapore as being those of civil society and democratization in the region. She saw her role as that of attempting to open up the level of debate. She felt that the level of discussion tends to stay very much within given frames, and thus does not look at the fundamentals that are constraining individuals.

I asked her whether she saw the greatest advances being made within Singapore, as regards gender issues, coming from NGOs, like AWARE (Association of Women for Action and Research) which has a high level of activism around gender issues, or more specifically through the role of women politicians, in advancing political and social issues for women. She responded as follows:

In the first place I wouldn't say that AWARE is the only one of its kind ... In Singapore there are a variety of groups that have surfaced, many of them informal groups. Some of them may not even recognize [what they are saying] as feminism, but if you listen to what is being said, it really is feminist in its orientation, feminist in its politics insofar as it is making some demands for greater gender egalitarianism. As for the role that AWARE plays, in a direct political fashion, I think right now it is still very insufficient. It's still beginning to raise its head once again. And my personal position is that ... and I've said this publicly before, I'm not really concerned with the number of women politicians in parliament, because it doesn't necessarily work for women. Because the issue is not so much whether there are women in parliament, there are women in politics. The issue is what are these women saying. And I think one of the positions AWARE took in its earlier days, was to push for the expansion of women in politics. But you can't do that without clarifying that what you're looking for, is women that speak for women, and how can you speak for women if you are still working within the dominant patriarchal mould of debate. And that's why I thought for me, my direction therefore is to start trying to reshape the debate. And I see that as the most crucial role AWARE can play. They need to turn their attention to their members, I think they now have four hundred or five hundred members, it can turn its attention to them, get them to start, in a sense unsilencing themselves, because despite its large numbers, you find very few women from within AWARE really speak up, or even are involved in AWARE activities ... So, then when you pick a political representative, no matter what party you are, you've got to pick representatives, who are listening to the politicized women, and what they are saying. There has to be some kind of alignment.

This Associate Professor has written widely in the area of gender, class and ethnicity and I asked her about her views on the intersection of gender and class in Singapore. 'Well if you look at political issues, you can never take class away from them. Now, often it is the middle class women, who have the resources, particularly the language resources, to stand up and make claims and make demands upon the state, upon the government.' She also made the point that middle class women are also the ones that have careers, and employ foreign domestic maids, and she argued that this made them open to the charge of collusion with patriarchalism and so she felt that these women had to be continuously critical of their situation. She herself employed a live-in domestic maid, and had been criticized for espousing feminist principles, and employing a woman to work for her. She commented as follows:

> It was much simpler when I did not have children to look after. So how is a woman going to cope with all this particularly in a situation like Singapore where you have insufficient crèches, and even if you do have crèches and day-care centres, I have got reservations about putting my child in there because of the multi-racial policy, and how that translates sometimes into racial discrimination, inadvertently or otherwise.

She felt that this was a case in point of the intersection of class and politics, because many middle class members of AWARE, employ foreign domestic maids, who have really no employment rights or protection in Singapore, and she noted they've attempted to actually push the government towards having at least minimum labour legislation, in terms of working conditions, hours of work, pay and so on.

'On Being Political'

I asked this Associate Professor how she would like to see her role developing in the future as a spokesperson for both women's issues and the bigger issues of civil society. I asked her whether she would see herself moving into the political arena in some context. She responded as follows:

> I think everything is political. And so, I see, once you are a citizen you are a political creature. Whether you speak, or whether you don't speak, whether you speak within a dominant discourse, whether you don't, I mean it is about politics. And so I think there is a much more serious view of politics. As for me being a spokesperson, I don't see myself as a spokesperson. In fact, one of the things that I am disturbed about is the tendency to turn to certain people as experts.

For her the issue was not so much being defined as an expert, or a spokesperson, but of opening up the debate around the notion of the civil society. She felt that it was about encouraging people how to *think* – outside of received knowledge, to encourage people to debate and take different positions. I asked her how this position squared with the position of the government on the development of 'talent', 'creativity', and 'quality people' for the future success and prosperity of Singapore. She responded as follows:

> There is a recognition that there is insufficient creativity, they are the two buzz words now, that come from the government, that you cannot think in boxes, and that we should introduce creative thinking in the schools. So there's a concern with these issues because of the global economy. And I think Singapore is particularly sensitive to that, because we are a city state, and we became a city state out of an historical event. It wasn't even out of choice really; it was expulsion from Malaysia. And that changed our economic base, our economic considerations, our economic priorities, and therefore our programmes and policies overnight. So I have to emphasize that I'm sympathetic with the government's position insofar as how you deal with larger economic questions which are also germane to your survival as a nation, given the fact that we're a city state our resources are not just the people of Singapore, our resources are also really the resources of our neighbours and therefore our relationships with our neighbours etc. And given the volatility of the political situation here, you cannot afford to continue with the kind of education where people do not learn flexibility of position, even political positions ... The thing about this government is that it does have its ears and eyes open, it does have certain understanding of the scenarios.

Career as an Index of Identity

I asked this Associate Professor what global and social changes were occurring which she thought might advance the position of women in Singapore. She responded as follows:

> I think the biggest social change, is that more and more women are turning to careers as an index of their identities. And therefore in relation to that, they do not fundamentally question patriarchy ... that they are accepting certain values that actually fundamentally devalue the feminine. Now in effect, when they make that kind of decision they're really voting with their bodies, in the full sense of the word. Because as you know in the context of Singapore, a prime consideration currently is the whole demographic issue that women are not marrying early enough, they're not producing children, and so on. Particularly women of the middle classes, because there is a certain underlying eugenics position here. And the belief that particular groups would, should, be procreating more than others, because they are qualitatively better. And this then does put a certain pressure on the government because how do you deal with that situation.

She made the point that women in Singapore are seen as having the resources to make more choices and that Singapore women are seen in the region as '... too demanding, too liberated. Interestingly not because they're liberated in a feminist sense of the word, but because through cultural spread of certain kinds of icons, certain lifestyles, they expect a different kind of relationship with their husband.' She claimed that, as a result of this, women in Singapore are seen to have lost their 'Asian edge'. However she thought that women in Singapore were under pressure, because of the threat of extra-marital affairs, and being too demanding and this, she argued, had the effect of making them more submissive, and docile than they might otherwise be.

I suggested that women in Singapore, particularly middle class women, are so well educated, and many of them educated overseas, that they had the ability to play the game of buying into the requisite notion of 'Asianness' but at the same time having a firm grasp of their own position in the world. Certainly many young Singaporean women are very affluent, and I argued that they have a very different set of options and perspectives around choices, and it puts them in a group that does define Singapore as being very different within the Southeast Asian context, in relation to other women. In response, she felt that the reality was that there was no single group of women in Singapore, even amongst middle class women, she felt it was a very variable group and that they actively pursue different choices. She argued that there are elements of this group who would not submit to any aspect of the Asianist ethos, and would respond in a very different kind of way.

> They would say that the Singaporean man is old fashioned, and they do not want to have anything to do with them, and they look for husbands outside ... just like the men who look for an orientalized female who they imagine can be found in other parts of Southeast Asia. The women do the same thing; they have a certain stereotype of the western man being more liberated. And interestingly that stereotype works in a funny way, because the Singaporean women is in fact an ideal wife, within the paradigm of an orientalized woman, because she has the sophistication that allows her to enter into 'the white world', the European world and the American world, and yet she also brings with her the qualities of the exotic ... But having said that I must also say that it costs them. There are many women in Singapore, and I like to think I belong to this group, who do exert their independence, who know what they want, who do not conform to expectations, either the exotic Asian mould, or the exotic western mould, but who quite often select, who in fact see the variations possible as offering choices, and make their choices in relation to their feminist politics and positions.

Conclusion

The issue of global, social and economic change has been a significant theme throughout this book. This chapter has considered some of the global and social factors which impact on the position of women in leadership positions in Hong Kong and Singapore. It has also considered the contribution of women 'opinion-leaders' in Hong Kong and Singapore in shaping the debate around gender, and social change. Economic, political and social changes impact on legislative and policy changes which in turn impact on the position of women in these societies. As has been shown the direction of such debates are important for the future growth of Hong Kong and Singapore. In terms of global issues, the growth of the 'new economies', and the global knowledge economy are seen as positive developments for professional women, although not necessarily for other groups of women. Legislation supporting anti-discrimination and equal opportunities was seen as offering significant advancement, as well as education and the growth of global trade. This has become a factor in Hong Kong life, but as yet the Singapore government remains resistant to anti-discrimination legislation. Women 'opinion-leaders' in Hong Kong and Singapore understood the significance of 'the political' within the debate, whether this involved policy formulation and the development of new legislative ordinances, or whether it involved a direct political role in Cabinet or in the Legislative Council in Hong Kong, or whether it involved leading a policy think-tank to act in a lobbying capacity, or whether it involved being a spokesperson on gender and other related issues.

Conclusion

The chapters of this book have examined a number of issues concerned with questions of globalization, gender and changing work cultures in Asia. More particularly the book has explored the impact of the new economy on the relationship between gender and specific professional labour markets in two global cities, Hong Kong and Singapore. The debates have been contexualized more broadly within the framework of globalization, gender and social change in Asia. What conclusions can be drawn from the findings and analysis of the issues raised in this research? Analysis has operated at a macro level of globalization, in terms of political, economic and social change and changing patterns of labour migration, and at a micro level, in terms of the impact of such changes on professional women in organizational and social life. At a macro level the questions raised by this book include: What are the implications for gendered labour markets of globalization and the growth of the new economy? Does globalization and the growth of the global knowledge economy present new opportunities for professional women? What implications does the growth of the new economy have on transnational labour markets? The key issues around which analysis has taken place are as follows:

- Globalization, gendered labour markets and the transmigration of labour.
- Equal Opportunities and equity in gender differentiated labour markets.
- The implications of demographics and its impact on state policy, and on single and married women.
- The role of foreign migrant labour in serving the needs of advanced economies.
- Career opportunities and organizational constraints for professional women.
- Leadership and management issues for professional women.
- Personal and social issues confronting professional women.
- Does globalization and the growth of the new economy present new opportunities for professional women?

Globalization, gendered labour markets and the transmigration of labour

Globalization has led to a number of processes that are significant in redefining the nature of local economies and work cultures. Globalization has led to the growth of global cities, such as Hong Kong and Singapore, and to the growth of the global knowledge economy, with work cultures and work identities being redefined to meet the needs of the global knowledge economy. Corporate restructuring has been a central feature of globalization, as has the process of the transmigration of labour. Transnationalization of labour regimes now characterize both professional workforces, and service workers who frequently supply the support structures necessary for the maintenance of global cities, and the global professionals who form a large part of the workforce of these global cities.

The theorization of globalization has been shown to be overly economistic, ignoring the gendered implications of these new types of labour market segmentation. Sassen (1998) has shown the strategic importance of gender within these regimes in relation to the restructuring of labour markets, and the feminization of employment within a highly differentiated division of labour.

The global cities of Asia such as Hong Kong and Singapore offer interesting examples of cities, where the dynamics of global capitalism and the specifics of Asian capitalism operate with a high degree of symmetry. What Nonini and Ong (1997) describe as 'flexible accumulation', encompasses labour processes, labour markets, products and patterns of consumption operating together to produce patterns of organizational and societal change for these cities and their workers. As Tyner (2001) observes the process of economic restructuring accompanying globalization is characterized by a more highly differentiated division of labour on the basis of ethnicity, gender and geography. Hong Kong and Singapore have the highest numbers of female professionals in Asia. The governments of Hong Kong and Singapore have consciously supported this differentiated division of labour through the adoption of an open-door policy, to attract both global talent and female migrant domestic labour. Both 'local' highly paid professionals as well as 'global talent' rely on foreign migrants to service their professional lives. Outside of these transnational migrants remain large numbers of far less well educated populations, who also create an asymmetry in labour markets.

Government policies, while supporting the influx of these groups of foreign domestic workers, provide them with few civil rights. More generally there is little commitment to gender ideology in many of the countries in the region, and the GDI (Gender Sensitive Development Index) is lower than the HDI (Human Development Index). The 'national agenda' of countries in the region, including Hong Kong and Singapore, overshadows the gender agenda. The recent down turn in the economies of Hong Kong and Singapore has already reinforced the national conservatism of these countries and the backlash is already being directed at women, and this is likely to be reinforced in the future.

Equal opportunities and equity in gender differentiated labour markets

One of the central and recurring issues raised throughout this book is, in the face of globalization, social change and an increasingly gender differentiated labour market, where do we locate the sites where issues around equal opportunities and equity are to be raised, particularly as has been noted elsewhere, when there is a lack of advocacy for women in the face of such changes (Bradley, 1993; Brooks and Mackinnon, 2001). Sassen (1998) identifies potential sites including the expansion of civil society, international law and human rights. However as I have pointed out earlier, this becomes difficult where countries have not become signatories to such international conventions, including human rights and equal employment opportunities such as the United Nations Convention on the Elimination of All Forms of Discrimination Against Women (CEDAW). The framing of legislation including anti-discrimination and human rights legislation is the *sine qua non* of a commitment by countries to equity and equal opportunities. It is also a fundamental element in the democratization process and the growth of civil society. Hong Kong has shown a commitment to the development of such policy and is a signatory to CEDAW, Singapore is not. The development of such a commitment through legislation is at a more advanced stage in Hong Kong than Singapore, although the future direction of policy and practice in both countries remains uncertain.

Hong Kong prior to 1997 showed a commitment to anti-discrimination policy in both legislative terms and in terms of institutional equality, even if not in its informal structures. The enactment of the Bill of Rights Ordinance in 1991 in Hong Kong identified equality as a human right and thus paved the way for anti-discrimination legislation. The Sex Discrimination Ordinance was enacted in 1995, which led to the establishment of an Equal Opportunities Commission. Such legislation while far reaching, does not always translate into organizational policy and practices, and institutional equality usually lags behind legislation. However this is a significant commitment by Hong Kong at a high level, to principles of equal opportunities and equity.

Singapore, as has been shown, is not a signatory to CEDAW and the issue of equal opportunities and equity has not, until recently, been addressed. There is only limited public debate on these issues and the position of the Singapore government has traditionally been that as the financial responsibility for the family is in the husband/father's hands, then there can be no equal opportunities. There is little in the way of opposition to these issues in Singapore, and there is no clear indication of any government commitment to equal opportunities or equity.

Implications of demographics on state policy and on single and married women

The global cities of Hong Kong and Singapore show demographic patterns which parallel most other advanced societies, particularly where middle class communities are concerned including: a decline in patterns of fertility for professional women; an increase in divorce, and in the number of female headed households; an increase in the number of single professional women; an increase in the number of professional women holding senior positions; a delay in the age of marriage for women and men; a dramatic increase in the number of women in the workforce. In addition an increase in the number of women in tertiary education and a direct relationship between levels of education and women holding professional positions.

Hong Kong and Singapore are characterized by high levels of literacy and education. There is a pattern of 'marrying down' in Singapore, where older and well established men marry less well educated and less financially well established women. This pattern does not exist in Hong Kong and men tend to marry women of equal social standing and education. Hence the emphasis in Hong Kong on women undertaking tertiary education is stimulated at least in part by the desire to marry a well educated and rich husband. The media in Hong Kong and Singapore have been giving a lot of attention to the issue of single professional women recently, and this could be seen as part of the backlash against the success of women economically. There has been a tendency within the media to focus on the fact that Hong Kong professional women are too selective in their choice of marriage partner and also to show how women professionals are experiencing harassment in their workplaces and are too worried about losing their jobs to complain.

The Singapore government has long been concerned with the numbers of unmarried, middle-class Chinese women, as well as with the numbers of children, middle-class Chinese women are having. It has adopted a selective pro-natalist population policy, encouraging this group of women to have more children. The government has also sponsored matchmaking units to encourage singles to meet suitable partners. As indicated they have also resolutely rejected equal opportunities policy.

The role of foreign migrant labour in serving the needs of advanced economies

The research has raised a number of issues around the position of foreign migrant domestic labour. This is a global phenomenon and foreign domestic labour is particularly pronounced in such global cities as Hong Kong and Singapore. This development has clearly assisted professional women in these cities that also show the highest number of professional women workers in Asia. Questions raised include to what extent are opportunities for professional women in Hong Kong and Singapore facilitated by foreign migrant labour? What are the rights and conditions of work for foreign domestic labourers in Hong Kong and Singapore? To what extent does foreign migrant labour offset the needs for organizations to provide childcare facilities for their employees?

It has been shown that an impact of globalization has been the transmigration of labour supply, particularly the movement of young women from countries such as Indonesia, Philippines, Sri Lanka and Thailand to act as foreign domestic labour for professionals in global cities such as Hong Kong and Singapore. The state has intervened directly in Hong Kong and Singapore to control the supply of labour. In Hong Kong there is no specific legislation covering the employment of foreign domestic workers, and in theory they work under the same employment ordinances as local workers. However their position makes them vulnerable to discrimination and they are frequently exploited by employers and agencies.

Foreign domestic workers in Singapore, as has been shown, are given no legal protection in employment terms, and are the subject of restrictive immigration legislation, which is also degrading and constitutes gender discrimination. Because of their unprotected position, foreign domestic workers in Singapore are the subjects of considerable abuse, even murder, which is unlikely to change until a legislative framework is put in place to protect the rights of such workers.

Career opportunities and organizational constraints for professional women

Research has shown that organizations remain somewhat 'hostile environments' to women and pose organizational constraints to women's career opportunities. It has also been shown that organizations are 'masculinist' in character and orientation, and maintain an exclusivity as regards the entry of women to senior positions. So what are the findings of this research as regards career opportunities and organizational constraints for professional women in the face of corporate restructuring and organizational change? It has been argued that some of the advantages of globalization and the global knowledge economy has created more opportunities for women, and a new climate, more open, transparent and accountable, which could facilitate the movement of women into senior positions.

The findings of this research show that the experiences of organizational life in Hong Kong and Singapore parallel the experiences of professional women in other countries. Despite the strong commitment of both countries to the global knowledge economy, and the accompanying expansion of opportunities, there is very little evidence of opportunities being translated into any tangible form for professional women. The experiences of academic women in Hong Kong and Singapore reveal the same opportunities and obstacles experienced by academics in the UK and Australia. The corporate restructuring of academic life and its impact on issues of equal opportunities and equity reveal many of the same constraints on career opportunities for professional women as exist elsewhere. Women in corporate life have not reached a critical mass in Singapore, while in both Hong Kong and Singapore the close links between business and family have created more opportunities for women to reach higher levels of corporate life.

This research revealed some interesting differences between corporate and academic life in terms of opportunities for professional women, as I have noted elsewhere (Brooks, 2001a). Academic life appears to afford academic women fewer opportunities to get to the top of organizational structures. Corporate life appears to accommodate change more rapidly than academic life, and to recognize and reward successful women in a way that academic institutions do not. The existence of legislation that means the experience of discrimination can be tested in the courts gives professional women in Hong Kong significant advantage over professional women in Singapore. Women in corporate life in Hong Kong were self-confident and used to occupying decision-making roles and taking on leadership positions. In some cases professional women in Hong Kong occupied a 'dual-career' position with highly successful political and corporate career profiles.

Academic women in Hong Kong and Singapore, at least from the findings of this research, are, in many cases, redefining their identities and are often not seeking positions at the top of academia, but seeking instead intrinsic satisfaction from their work. On a personal level many are now seeking more in terms of quality of life, rather than purely career satisfaction. Academic and corporate women are diversifying in career terms, seeking different avenues in terms of personal satisfaction, be this changing career directions, moving into different types or areas of work, and giving more attention to relationships.

Gender politics, as a feature of organizational life, was something that had been experienced by some, but not all, professional women involved in the research. Some women were more conscious or sensitized to gender politics, and thus could identify aspects of such behavior more readily. Some academic women, in particular, had been directly concerned with legislation or organizational politics which addressed aspects of discriminatory behaviour as it emerged in an institutional context.

The redefining of professional identity in the career ambitions of many of the professional women is reflected in issues around promotion. Uniformity within organizations around promotion appears not to exist even within organizational types, for example universities or corporations. It has been argued during the last ten years that a greater emphasis has been placed on transparency and accountability of operations. However it is clear from the findings of this research, that promotion and its accompanying structures remains problematic for professional women. It is difficult to make comparison between organizations even within Hong Kong or Singapore, and comparison between countries is virtually impossible. Different organizations follow different 'national models', for example an American model, a British model, or even a 'hybrid' model, with an attempt to combine both. It results in both academic and corporate positions carrying little meaning in a global context, with some positions carrying seriously 'elevated' titles. The global restructuring of corporations and universities has resulted in some strange anomalies arising.

The findings of this research show a large degree of disaffection, particularly among academic women with the promotion system of universities. Many of the professional women interviewed in this research were satisfied with the remuneration system and found satisfaction in the intrinsic rewards offered by the job, as opposed to seeking to climb the career ladder. Many had decided that quality of life issues were as important as career issues, and actively made decisions to give priority to the former. Corporate women allied themselves more closely in terms of career and ambition with the success of the organization, and defined their success far more in organizational terms than did academic women. In the case of corporate women, individual success was closely allied to corporate success. This was reflected in aspirational differences, particularly in relation to the position they would like to achieve in the organization. Academic life clearly no longer holds the appeal for academic women that it once did in career terms.

Apart from the specific nature of the organization and organizational constraints, a number of factors were identified as hampering career development. These included personal issues such as children and family, individual failings such as intolerance or the inability to speak Chinese, to factors such as racism, in the case of Hong Kong, or the 'culture of fear' as in the case of Singapore. Other organizational related factors included the incompetency of support staff, and the poor quality of management. There were few organizational factors which were seen to benefit professional women, but a number of factors were identified as assisting career opportunities, these included the ability to write academically, being single, having drive and the personality to succeed, having the opportunity to work with influential women opinion-leaders in Hong Kong and the advantage of being a woman in a man's world.

Leadership and management issues for professional women

Leadership and management are now seen as centrally important concepts in the academic as well as corporate worlds. The growth of the global knowledge economy and the redefining of knowledge and 'knowledge workers' (of various types) as commodities in this process has led to a fusion of corporate and academic languages, principles of operation, and conceptions of management. In addition, academia now shares with the corporate world the experience of corporate downsizing.

Women in management and leadership in Asia have traditionally faced a number of cultural barriers, yet the familial structures of much Asian business has in fact benefited many women who occupy leading positions in the business world. The findings of this research show women as confident, capable leaders who have a clear sense of what being a manager, and being a woman manager, means. Women in corporate and academic life defined their management roles as team builders, facilitators and conciliators. However, corporate leaders very much defined people development as intrinsic to organizational success, as opposed to the more liberal humanistic position, adopted by women managers in academia, as developing the potential of the individual. Persuasion and discussion were seen as important for corporate and academic contexts, although it was quite clear that such discussion needed to lead to decision-making.

This research shows that traditional negative stereotypes about women's qualities as leaders and managers still exist, although women managers are also defined in very positive terms. Professional women made clear distinctions in what they saw as the qualities that women and men bring to the managerial role. Overall women were seen as having to work harder and prove themselves more often. Only a small number of the professional women interviewed applied a gender analysis of organizational life to attempt to explain some of the distinctions. Where such an analysis was applied, professional women understood the issues around organizations privileging the 'masculine' over the 'feminine'. Some women felt that gender should not be seen as a factor in leadership, and that leadership qualities should be gender-neutral, however others recognized that gender politics is a fact of life within organizational structures, and inevitably impacts on women leaders. Many recognized that for women to get to the top as leaders they had to have exceptional qualities in leadership terms, unlike men, who reached these positions with often very mediocre qualities.

Women professionals in Hong Kong in both corporate and academic contexts seemed more conscious of the dynamics of gender politics within organizational structures, whereas many of the professional women in Singapore, but certainly not all, seemed reluctant to apply a gender analysis. This could be the result of over a decade of discussion in Hong Kong around human rights, equity and equal opportunities, and the impact of the introduction of significant legislation in the area. The absence of both discussion and legislation in Singapore has created an environment where only organizational spokespersons such as those emerging from groups like AWARE are prepared to speak out.

Leadership is not an easy concept to identify or define and it is clear from the findings of this research that leadership can be seen in formal and informal terms. Leadership is seen as something that is an attribute or quality held by certain individuals, or something that is defined within a formal position or title. What is clear from this research is that leadership is defined as distinct from management, where management is seen as instrumental in character, leadership is seen as characterized by vision, and an ability to carry the confidence of others in the leader's ability. The research findings show that many women in positions of leadership were, in their own terms, reluctant leaders, or in a position of leadership by default. Leadership in a formal sense is understood as the ability to bring through decisions that are regarded as successful for the organization and supported by staff. Leadership in an informal sense is where individuals carry the confidence of their peers, because of their ability to speak out on issues that are significant in terms of equity and social justice. At times there is a fundamental incompatibility between these positions, and hence the reluctance of some women to assume a leadership mantle. In some cases, these two positions did coincide and in those cases, both the organization and its personnel benefited. Examples of such women leaders were apparent in the corporate and academic world.

Findings from this research show the relative absence of women role models in the corporate and academic world in Hong Kong and Singapore. This does not result from the fact that women do not make good role models, but from the paucity of women in positions of leadership either historically or contemporaneously. The research findings also show that in comparing management styles, women managers have had little opportunity, to date, to develop styles which are distinctive, and which reflect different priorities, because it requires re-education in terms of management training and organizational thinking. Traditional patterns of management, dominated by masculinist attitudes and priorities, remains a feature of corporate and academic life and it could remain the case until women form a critical mass in management and leadership terms. It is not therefore surprising that the findings of this research show that few women defined or attempted to implement new management styles, or indeed had any experience of innovative management styles. There appeared to be a lack of reflexivity regarding philosophies of management, and leadership, and an emphasis on the pragmatics of dealing with decisions on an issue by issue basis. The conclusion reached from the findings of this research on issues of gender management and leadership is that more research is needed on the development of new and innovative management styles for women.

Personal and social issues confronting professional women

Professional women in Hong Kong and Singapore face a range of personal and social issues confronting women in many cities facing rapid economic, political and social change. However, the fact that Hong Kong and Singapore are both Chinese cities presents a number of additional challenges for professional women. These challenges are faced by both Chinese and other local groupings, as well as expatriate professionals, and can be seen as gender issues as opposed to issues of race or ethnicity. There are cultural pressures emanating from Chinese culture, particularly the emphasis on marriage and children, and also the issue of 'filial piety', which defines familial obligations and responsibilities very clearly. There is clear resistance to these traditional pressures and the adoption of different patterns including co-habitation, and decisions to give career issues predominance over those of procreation. However, the pressures are clearly exerted by both family and, in the case of Singapore, by the state.

Findings from the research show that in the face of the on-going economic downturn and recession in Hong Kong and Singapore, there is a backlash against women, particularly successful professional women, with the media reporting how professional women are being abused at work, and how women are being encouraged to be less discriminating in their choice of marriage partner. There is also pressure from television soap operas to show how career women are 'neglecting' husband and home, and indirectly leading to divorce. In Singapore pressure is being brought to bear on single, professional, childless women and the emphasis is put on the loneliness of being single.

Professional women remained pragmatic in the face of such pressures, motivated as much by materialism as ambition. Professional women in this research, and more generally in Hong Kong and Singapore, have an advantage over their peers in other countries in the ready accessibility of foreign domestic 'live-in' labour. In many cases two foreign maids were employed. This has allowed professional women a much higher level of professional and personal freedom than their counterparts in the UK, Canada and Australia.

Findings from this research showed that on the issue of marriage vs. being single, the stereotype of the single career oriented woman of the 1990s is more the exception than the rule. Both single and married women emerged as highly successful in this research. While both single and married professional women in Hong Kong and Singapore were focused on their work and careers, this was not to the exclusion of other aspects of life. Most had reflected on how to accommodate the needs and careers of partners/husbands, and were prepared to make changes to accommodate them. Those who were single did not see their careers as playing a part in why they remain single, but had come to terms with the situation, and did not actively seek to change it. Age seemed to preoccupy women in Singapore more than professional women in Hong Kong, and single professional women in Singapore appeared more conservative as regards issues such as co-habitation. Both single and married women, with or without children, had given considerable thought to whether or not to have children, and how children might impact on both lifestyle and career. Several single professional women in Hong Kong and Singapore had reconciled themselves to not having children or to adoption. Where women did have children, then without exception, a 'live-in' domestic maid provided the support. Regardless of this, finding symmetry between family and career proved difficult for most women.

Another stereotype, which, from the findings of this research was found to have no real basis, is that of the successful careerist who prioritizes career over that of family or partner's career. This research shows that professional women have a more open attitude to both their own career and that of their partner, being prepared to accommodate their partner's career, and even move countries if their partner's career required this. I have made the point in this research that having reached a certain point in their careers, professional women are now giving more consideration to quality of life issues. However the point should be made here that this did not imply that professional women were less interested in their careers, only that they were prepared to diversify if the situation required this. Many couples had influenced one another in terms of doctoral research, or areas of work, which had often led to improvements in relationships. There appeared to be little or no competition between spouses in career terms.

As regards spousal attitudes towards parenting/childcare issues, most professional women aspired to an equal role in parenting, but few really achieved this. Most of the households had at least one 'live-in' maid, particularly where children were young, and this neutralized potential difficulties as regards childcare responsibilities. Despite this, most women in this research made their position regarding expectations very clear as far as their partner's responsibilities to childcare are concerned.

The findings of this research show that in terms of personal and social issues confronting professional women in Hong Kong and Singapore, the role of foreign domestic maids is a crucial one in facilitating successful careers and indeed partnerships. Where single professional women had familial obligations, which they frequently had to manage alone, the fact that 'live-in' foreign domestic maids were available provided crucial support services. The existence of such support gave professional women considerable freedom to pursue their careers and to pursue quality of life issues.

Does globalization and the growth of the new economy present new opportunities for professional women?

As has been shown, the growth of the new economy is an important factor in advancing opportunities for professional women. At the same time new patterns of inequality have emerged producing a highly differentiated labour market characterized by ethnicity and gender. A number of global issues were identified in this research as advancing the position of women into leadership and management. The growth of the global knowledge economy and the implications of the new economy in opening up possibilities for women have both positive and negative consequences. The potential for increased flexibility in terms of hours of work and the ability to work from home, does not seem to be fully recognized by organizations, with professional women in this research describing issues such as 'visibility', as an on-going aspect of organizational life. In addition, the growth of the global knowledge economy is accompanied by a 'feminization' of business and management with professional women frequently occupying positions at lower levels of management. Certainly, women in the corporate sphere recognized that there were still relatively few women occupying senior corporate positions. Indeed when comparing the situation with countries such as Taiwan, Japan and Korea, the situation for women reaching the top of the corporate ladder seemed very limited.

Findings from this research show very clearly that legislation is a significant factor in leading to change. Legislation in itself will not change attitudes directly, but the existence of equal opportunities and anti-discrimination legislation does create an environment where potentially discriminatory attitudes can be tested in the courts. This is clearly the case in Hong Kong. However it is also clear that organizations, even where equal opportunities positions have been established, are not necessarily pro-active in advancing gender or other issues. More specific policies emerging from organizational contexts could assist women in this regard.

In Hong Kong, the Bill of Rights Ordinance (1991) and the Sex Discrimination Ordinance (1995) were seen as major advances in legislative terms, but their impact in terms of the abolition of non-discriminatory practices remained some way off. In addition, since the return of Hong Kong to China in 1997, more traditional Chinese attitudes were re-emerging. This was considered to be more directly related to the economic downturn and unemployment in Hong Kong, leading to social pressures such as domestic violence and divorce. The 'backlash' against women at many levels has been documented by the media in Hong Kong and Singapore.

Education was identified as an important factor in advancing opportunities for women. Both Hong Kong and Singapore have high levels of education with significant numbers advancing to tertiary education. Women were not only more highly qualified but were moving into non-traditional areas. Hong Kong and Singapore have the highest number of professional women in Asia. Women at the very top of academic leadership structures within this research highlighted the choices women frequently had to make to get to the top. Even those at the top were making decisions based on personal and lifestyle issues and decisions about their life patterns.

One of the clear issues emerging from this research was that changing attitudes within organizational structures was seen as crucial to promoting the advancement of women into positions of management and leadership. Management within organizations does not necessarily carry any expertise or knowledge of equal opportunities or equity, and highlights the deficiencies of organizational structures. Central to this debate is the question of how gender issues are incorporated into organizational structures. It was recognize that women managers have more difficulty in raising gender related issues than do male managers. Another issue emerging from the research regarding organizational change was the acceptance of different models of leadership, which could allow greater mobility into leadership for women and overall an acceptance of different organizational styles. In addition, in organizations that are generally 'flat' structures (populated by women, in the main), promotion opportunities become somewhat elusive. It was suggested that 'benchmarking' might be a useful way to provide some comparisons with performance criteria in other organizations and thus provide more promotion opportunities.

The research identified a number of women who had made significant contributions to life in Hong Kong and Singapore, over and above a contribution to a specific organization. Several women identified in this research had made a huge contribution to political life, by providing an international forum for a number of debates, through publishing articles on issues around equal opportunities and academic freedom in Hong Kong, through the development of anti-discrimination legislation, to serving on government committees and in the Legislative Council in Hong Kong. Their contribution as fearless advocates of human rights and anti-discrimination has been outlined in the chapters. In Singapore also many women contributed actively to the debate about gender and civil society even if political office did not form an immediate part of their thinking. The contribution of women through policy initiatives and debates, through direct political involvement, through academic publications, or newspaper articles, all made a contribution to social and organizational change. Professional women in Hong Kong and Singapore understood the significance of 'the political' in these debates whatever expression it took. They are some of the many women making a difference and shaping the direction of social change by shaping the debate around gender, social and organizational change. Meeting these women, seeing them on CNN, and knowing they are out there, continuing to advocate for change, is an inspirational experience, and one that I hope has been conveyed and documented in a satisfactory way in the chapters of this book. These women have made and are continuing to make a difference, and the future of Hong Kong and Singapore based on principles of social justice and equity will owe much to the women represented in this book.

Bibliography

Adler, N. 'Competitive Frontiers: Women Managing Across Borders', in D.N. Izraeli and N.A. Adler (eds), *Competitive Frontiers: Women Managers in a Global Economy* (Oxford: Blackwell Publishers, 1994).

Adler, N. J. 'Women do not Want International Careers: And Other Myths about International Management', *Organization Dynamics*, 13(2) (1984): 66-79.

Alcid, M.L. 'Legal and Organizational Support Mechanisms for Foreign Domestic Workers', in N. Heyzer, G. Lycklama and N. Whereon (eds), *The Trade in Domestic Workers: Causes, Mechanisms and Consequences of International Migration*, Selected Papers from a Regional Policy Dialogue on Foreign Women Domestic Workers, Columbo, Sri Lanka, August 10-14, 1992 (Kuala Lumpur: Asian and Pacific Development Centre, 1994).

Allison, A. *Nightwork* (Chicago: University of Chicago Press, 1994).

Ang, I. and Stratton, J. 'Straddling East and West: Singapore's Paradoxical Search for a National Identity', in S. Perera (ed.), *Asia and Pacific Inscriptions* (Melbourne: Meridian Books, 1995).

Antal, A.B. and Izraeli, D.N. 'A Global Comparison of Women in Management: Women Managers in their Homelands and as Expatriates', in E.A. Fagenson (ed.), *Women in Management: Trends, Issues and Challenges in Managerial Diversity, Vol 4: Women in Work* (Newbury Park: Sage, 1993).

Arnold, M. and Lee, E. *Perceptions and Attitudes of Hong Kong Chinese Male Executives about Women in Management*, Paper presented at the Proceedings of the 3rd International Conference on Comparative Management, Taiwan, 1990.

Asian Wall Street Journal, 'The Agony and the Ecstasy', November 14-16, 2003: 1-4.

Basch, L., Schiller, N.G., and Blanc, C.S. *Nations Unbound: Transnational Projects, Postcolonial Predicaments and Deterritorialized Nation-States* (Amsterdam: Gordon and Breach Publishers, 1994).

Blackmore, J. and Sacks, J. 'Women Leaders in the Restructured University', in A. Brooks and A. Mackinnon (eds), *Gender and the Restructured University: Changing Management and Culture in Higher Education* (Buckingham: Open University Press, 2001).

Bradley, D. 'A Foot in the Door: Women in Employment, Education and Training in Australia', *Unicorn*, 19(1) (1993): 15-27.

Brewster, C. *The Management of Expatriates* (London: Kogan Page, 1991).

Brooks, A. *Women and the Family in Confucianist and Communist China*, Unpublished M.A. Thesis, Department of Sociology and Social Anthropology, University of Keele, United Kingdom (1985).

Brooks, A. 'Restructuring Bodies of Knowledge', in A. Brooks and A. Mackinnon (eds), *Gender and the Restructured University: Changing Management and Culture in Higher Education* (Buckingham: Open University Press, 2001a).

Brooks, A. *The Intersection of Postcolonial, Feminist and Nationalist Discourses in Understanding Chinese Diasporic Communities*, Paper presented at the Conference of Asian Diasporas and Cultures: Globalisation, Hybridity, Intertextuality, Department of English Language and Literature, National University of Singapore, September 5-7, 2001 (Singapore: National University of Singapore, 2001b).

Brooks, A. 'The Uncertain Configurations of a Politics of Location in Southeast Asia: The Asian Family, Asian Values and Postcolonial Feminist Spaces', *Asian Journal of Social Sciences*, 31(1) (2003): 86-106.

Brooks, A. and Mackinnon, A. (eds) *Gender and the Restructured University: Changing Management and Culture in Higher Education* (Buckingham: Open University Press, 2001).

Castells, M. 'The University System: Engine of Development in the New World Economy', in J. Salmi and A. Verspoor (eds), *Revitalizing Higher Education* (London: Pergamon, 1994).

Castells, M. *The Rise of the Information Age, Volume 1: The Rise of the Network Society* (Oxford/Cambridge, Mass: Blackwell Publishers, 1996).

Castells, M. *End of Millennium: The Information Age, Volume 3* (Oxford: Blackwell Publishers, 1998).

Chan, A. and Lee, J. 'Women Executives in a Newly Industrialized Economy: The Singapore Scenario', in N.J. Adler and D.N. Izraeli (eds), *Competitive Frontiers: Women Managers in a Global Economy* (Oxford: Blackwell Publishers, 1994).

Chan, J. 'The Status of Women in a Patriarchal State: The Case of Singapore', in L. Edwards and M. Roces (eds), *Women in Asia: Tradition, Modernity and Globalization* (St Leonards, NSW: Allen and Unwin, 2000).

Chang, P. 'The Gender Division of Labour at Work', *Korean Women and Work* (Seoul: Asia Centre for Women's Studies, 1998).

Cheng, S.A. 'Migrant Women Domestic Workers in Hong Kong, Singapore and Taiwan: A Comparative Analysis', *Asian and Pacific Migration Journal*, 5(1) (1996): 139-152.

Cheung, F.M. (ed.) *Engendering Hong Kong Society* (Hong Kong: The Chinese University Press, 1997).

Chiang, L.H-N. 'Women in Taiwan: Linking Economic Prosperity and Women's Progress', in L. Edwards and M. Roces (eds), *Women in Asia: Tradition, Modernity and Globalization* (St Leonards, NSW: Allen and Unwin, 2000).

Chin, C. *In Service and In Servitude: Foreign Female Domestic Workers and the Malaysian 'Modernity' Project* (New York: Columbia University Press, 1998).

Collinson, D. and Hearn, J. 'Breaking the Silence on Men, Masculinities and Management', in D. Collinson and J. Hearn (eds), *Men as Managers, Managers as Men* (London: Sage, 1996).

Creighton, M. 'Marriage, Motherhood and Career Management in a Japanese "Counter-Culture"', in A. Imamura (ed.), *Re-Imagining Japanese Women* (Berkeley: University of California Press, 1996).

De Leon, C.T. and Ho, S. 'The Third Identity of Modern Chinese Women: Women Managers in Hong Kong', in D.N. Izraeli and N.A. Adler (eds), *Competitive Frontiers: Women Managers in a Global Economy* (Oxford: Blackwell Publishers, 1994).

Edwards, L. 'Women in the People's Republic of China: New Challenges to the Grand Gender Narrative', in L. Edwards and M. Roces (eds), *Women In Asia: Tradition, Modernity and Globalization* (St Leonards, NSW: Allen and Unwin, 2000).

Fagan, C. and Burchell, B. *European Foundation of Living and Working Conditions: Gender, Jobs and Working Conditions in the European Union* (Luxembourg: Office for Official Publications of the European Community, 2002).

Far Eastern Economic Review, September 25, 2003, 6.

Featherstone, M. and Lash, S. 'Globalization, Modernity and the Spatialization of Social Theory: An Introduction', in M. Feathersone, S. Lash and R. Robertson (eds), *Global Modernities* (London: Sage, 1995).

Featherstone, M., Lash, S. and Robertson, R. (eds) *Global Modernities* (London: Sage, 1995).

Ghai, Y. 'Rights, Social Justice and Globalisation in East Asia', in J.R. Bauer and D.B. Bell (eds), *The East-Asian Challenge for Human Rights* (Cambridge: Cambridge University Press, 1999).

Green, F., Ashton, D., James, D. and Sung, J. 'The Role of the State in Skill Formation: Evidence from the Republic of Korea, Singapore, and Taiwan', *Oxford Review of Economic Policy*, 15(1) (1999): 82-95.

Hampson, S. 'Rhetoric or Reality? Contesting Definitions of Women in Korea', in L. Edwards and M. Roces (eds), *Women in Asia: Tradition, Modernity and Globalization* (St Leonards, NSW: Allen and Unwin, 2000).

Harris, H. 'Women in International Management: The Times they are a Changing?', *International Review of Women and Leadership*, 4(2) (1998): 6-11.

Harvey, D. *The Condition of Postmodernity: An Enquiry into the Origins of Cultural Change* (Oxford: Blackwell, 1993).

Hearn, J. 'Changing Men and Changing Management: Social Change, Social Research and Social Action', in M. Davidson and R. Burke (eds), *Women in Management: Current Research Issues* (London: Paul Chapman, 1994).

Hearn, J. 'Men, Managers and Management: The Case of Higher Education', in S. Whitehead and R. Moodey (eds), *Transforming Managers: Engendering Change in the Public Sector* (London: Taylor Francis, 1998).

Hearn, J. 'Academia, Management and Men: Making the Connections, Exploring the Implications', in A. Brooks and A. McKinnon (eds), *Gender and the Restructured University: Changing Management and Culture in Higher Education* (Buckingham: Open University Press, 2001).

Hearn, J. and Morgan, D. (eds) *Men, Masculinities and Social Theory* (London/ Boston: Unwin Hyman, 1990).

Heng, G. 'A Great Way to Fly: Nationalism, the State and Varieties of Third World Feminism', in M.J. Alexander and C.T. Mohanty (eds), *Feminist Genealogies, Colonial Legacies, Democratic Futures* (New York/London: Routledge, 1997).

Heng, G. and Devan, J. 'State Fatherhood: The Politics of Nationalism, Sexuality and Race', in A. Ong and M.G. Peletz (eds), *Bewitching Women, Pious Men, Gender and Body Politics in Southeast Asia* (Berkeley: University of California Press, 1995).

Heyzer, N. *Working Women in Southeast Asia: Development, Subordination, Emancipation* (Philadelphia: Open University Press, 1986).

Heyzer, N. 'The Internationalisation of Women's Work', *Southeast Asian Journal of Social Science*, 7(2) (1989): 25-40.

Heyzer, N. and Wee, V. 'Domestic Workers in Transient Overseas Employment: Who Benefits, Who Profits?', in N. Heyzer, G. Lycklama, A. Niejholt and N. Weerakoon (eds), *The Trade in Domestic Workers: Causes, Mechanisms and Consequences of International Migration, Vol.1*, Selected Papers from a Regional Policy Dialogue on Foreign Women Domestic Workers: International Migration, Employment and National Policies, Columbo, Sri Lanka, August 10-14, 1992, 31-102 (London: Zed Books, 1994).

Hochschild, A. *The Time Bind* (New York: Metropolitan Books, 1997).

Hochschild, A. 'Global Care-chains and Emotional Surplus Value', in W. Hutton and A. Giddens (eds), *On the Edge: Living with Global Capitalism* (London: Jonathan Cape, 2000).

Huang, S. and Yeoh, B. 'Ties that Bind: State Policy and Migrant Female Domestic Helpers in Singapore', *Geoforum*, 27(4) (1996): 479-493.

Huang, S. and Yeoh, B. 'The Difference Gender Makes: State, Policy and Contract Migrant Workers in Singapore', *Asian and Pacific Migration Journal*, 12(1-2) (2003): 75-97.

Izraeli, D.N. and Adler, N.A. (eds), *Competitive Frontiers: Women Managers in a Global Economy* (Oxford: Blackwell Publishers, 1994).

Jones, D. 'Knowledge Workers "R" Us: Academics, Practitioners and "Specific Intellectuals"', in C. Prichard, R. Hill, M. Chumer and H. Wilmot (eds), *Managing Knowledge: Critical Investigations of Work and Learning* (Basingstoke: Macmillan, 2000).

Joyner, K. and Preston, A. 'Gender Difference in Perceptions of Leadership Role, Performance and Culture in a University: A Case Study', *International Review of Women and Leadership*, 4(2) (1998): 34-43.

Lash, S. and Urry, J. *Economics of Signs and Space* (London: Sage,1994).

Law, W.-W. 'The Accommodation and Resistance to the Decolonisation, Neocolonisation and Recolonisation of Higher Education in Hong Kong', in M. Bray and W.O. Lee (eds), *Education and Political Transition: Implications of Hong Kong's Change of Sovereignty* (Hong Kong: Hong Kong University Press, 1997).

Lee, S. 'Issues in Research on Women, International Migration and Labour', in G. Battistella and A. Paganoni (eds), *Asian Women in Migration* (Quezon City: Scalabrini Immigration Centre, 1996).

Li, K.W. *Capitalist Development and Economism in East Asia: The Rise of Hong Kong, Singapore, Taiwan and South Korea* (London/New York: Routledge, 2002).

Li, X. and Zhang, X. 'Creating a Space for Women: Women's Studies in China in the 1980s', *Signs*, 20(1) (1994): 137-151.

Lyons, L. *Organizing for Domestic Worker Rights in Southeast Asia: Feminist Responses to Globalization*, Paper presented at the 15th Biennial Conference of the Asian Studies Association of Australia, Canberra, June 29-July 2, 2004.

McDowall, L. *Capital Culture: Gender at Work in the City* (Oxford: Blackwell, 1997).

Mackinnon, A. and Brooks, A. 'Introduction: Globalization, Academia and Change', in A. Brooks and A. Mackinnon (eds), *Gender and the Restructured University: Changing Management and Culture in Higher Education* (Buckingham: Open University Press, 2001).

Marceau, J. 'Australian Universities: A Contestable Future', in T. Coady (ed.), *Why Universities Matter: A Conversation about Values, Means and Directions* (Sydney: Allen and Unwin, 2000).

Marshall, J. *Women Managers Moving On* (London: Routledge, 1995).

Ngo, H.Y. 'Employment Status of Married Women in Hong Kong', *Sociological Perspectives*, 35(3) (1992): 475-488.

Nonini, D.M. and Ong, A. 'Chinese Transnationalism as an Alternative Modernity', in A. Ong and D. Nonini (eds), *Underground Empire: The Cultural Politics of Modern Chinese Transnationalism* (New York/London: Routledge, 1997).

Olivares, F. 'Women in Management in Italy: A Shifting Scenario', in N.J. Adler and D.N. Izraeli (eds), *Women in Management Worldwide*, 2nd edition (New York: M. E. Sharpe, 1992).

Ong, A. *Flexible Citizenship: The Cultural Logics of Transnationality* (Durham/London: Duke University Press, 1999).

Ong, C. 'Are S'pore women hitting boardroom glass ceiling?', *The Business Times*, March 16-17, 2002.

Pearson, V. 'Women in Hong Kong', in B.K.P. Leung (ed.) *Social Issues in Hong Kong* (Hong Kong/Oxford: Oxford University Press, 1990).

Perrons, D. *Globalization and Social Change* (London/New York: Routledge, 2004).

Petersen, C. 'Equality as a Human Right: The Development of Anti-Discrimination Law in Hong Kong', *Columbia Journal of Transnational Law*, 34(2) (1996): 335-388.

Petersen, C. 'Preserving Institutions of Autonomy in Hong Kong: The Impact of 1997 on Academia and the Legal Profession', *Southern Illinois Law Journal*, 22 (1998): 337-368.

Petersen, C. 'Implementing Equality: An Analysis of Two Recent Decisions under Hong Kong's Anti-Discrimination Laws', *Hong Kong Law Journal,* 29(2) (1999): 178-194.

Petersen, C. 'Equal Opportunities: A New Field of Law for Hong Kong', in C. Wacks (ed.), *Hong Kong's New Legal Order* (Hong Kong: Hong Kong University Press, 1999).

Petersen, C. 'Equal Pay for Work of Equal Value: A Feminist Perspective', in *Equal Pay for Work of Equal Value* (Hong Kong: Equal Opportunities Commission, 2000).

Petersen, C. 'The Law of Sexual Harassment in Hong Kong', in P. Tahmindjis (ed.), *The Law and Sexual Harassment: International, Domestic and Comparative Aspects* (Amsterdam: Kluwer, 2002).

Postiglione, G.A. 'Hong Kong's Universities Within the Global Academy', in G.A. Postiglione and J.T. Tang (eds), *Hong Kong's Reunion with China: Global Dimensions* (Hong Kong: Hong Kong University Press, 1997).

Pratt, G. 'From Registered Nurse to Registered Nanny: Discursive Geographies of Filipina Domestic Workers in Vancouver, B.C', *Economic Geography,* 75(3) (1999): 215-236.

Purushotam, N. 'Between Compliance and Resistance: Women and the Middle Class Way of Life in Singapore', in K. Sen and M. Stivens (eds), *Gender and Power in Affluent Asia* (London/New York: Routledge, 1998).

Republic of Korea (ROK) *Fourth Periodic Report of States of the Convention on the Elimination of All Forms of Discrimination Against Women, 1994-1997* (Seoul: Presidential Commission of Women's Affairs, 1998).

Reeves, R. *Happy Mondays: Putting the Pleasure Back into Work* (London: Momentum, 2001).

Reynolds, C. and Bennett, R. 'The Career Couple Challenge', *Personnel Journal,* (March 1991): 46-48.

Robertson, R. 'Globalization and Societal Modernization: A Note on Japan and Japanese Religion', *Sociological Analysis,* 47 (1987): 35-43.

Robertson. R. *Globalization* (London: Sage, 1992).

Robinson, K. *Marriage, Migration, Family Values and the 'Global Ecumene'.* Paper presented at the Migration and the 'Asian Family' in a Globalising World Conference, April 16-18, 2001 (Singapore: AsiaMetaCenter and the Centre for Advanced Studies, National University of Singapore, 2001).

Rosener, J. 'Ways Women Lead', *Harvard Business Review,* 68(8) (1990): 119-125.

Sassen, S. *The Mobility of Labour and Capital: A Study of International Investment and Labour Flow* (Cambridge: University of Cambridge, 1988).

Sassen, S. *Losing Control* (New York: Columbia University Press, 1996).

Sassen, S. *Globalization and its Discontents* (New York: The New Press, 1998).

Sharma, S. 'Psychology of Women in Management: A Distinct Feminine Leadership', *Equal Opportunities International,* 9(2) (1990): 13-18.

Slaughter, S. and Leslie, L. *Academic Capitalism: Politics, Policies and the Entrepreneurial University* (Baltimore: Johns Hopkins University Press, 1997).

Soin, K. 'Challenges for Women and Men in a Changing Environment', in D. Colome, Y. Meguro and T. Yamamoto (eds), *A Gender Agenda: Asia-Europe Dialogue* (Singapore: Japan Centre for International Exchange, 2001).

Standing, G. *Beyond the New Paternalism Basic Security as Equality* (London: Verso, 2002).

Stivens, M. 'Gender Politics and the Re-imagining of Human Rights in the Asia-Pacific', in A-M. Hilsdon, M. Macintyre, V. Mackie and M. Stevens (eds), *Human Rights and Gender Politics: Asia-Pacific Perspectives* (London/New York: Routledge, 2000).

Tacoli, C. 'International Migration and the Restructuring of Gender Asymmetries: Continuity and Change among Filipino Migrants in Rome', *International Migration Review*, 33 (Fall 1999): 658-659.

Tam, V.C.W. 'Foreign Domestic Helpers in Hong Kong and their Role in Childcare Provision', in J. H. Momsem (ed.), *Gender, Migration and Domestic Service* (London/New York: Routledge, 1999).

Thang, L.L., and Yu, W. 'Introduction: Assessing Women's Roles in Asian Economies', in L.L. Thang and W. Yu (eds), *Old Challenges, New Strategies: Women, Work and Family in Contemporary Asia* (Leiden/Boston: Brill Publishers, 2004).

The Straits Times 'HK men fear losing out to women in workplace', December 14, 2001.

The Straits Times 'Executives suffer rapes in silence to keep their jobs', March 5, 2002.

Thurow, L. 'Globalization: The Product of a Knowledge-Based Economy', *Annals of the American Academy of Political and Social Sciences*, 570 (2000): 19-31.

Tipton, E.K. 'Being Women in Japan, 1970-2000', in L. Edwards and M. Roces (eds), *Women in Asia: Tradition, Modernity and Globalization* (St Leonards, NSW: Allen and Unwin, 2000).

Toh, M.H. and Tay, B.N. *Households and Housing in Singapore, Census of Population 1990 Monograph: No 4* (Singapore: Census of Population Office, 1996).

Turner, B.S. (ed.) *Theories of Modernity and Postmodernity* (London: Sage, 1990).

Tyner, J.A. *The Production of Transnational Labor Migration and the Filipino Family: A Narrative*, Paper presented at the Migration and the 'Asian Family' in a Globalising World Conference, April 16-18, 2001 (Singapore: Asia MetaCentre and the Centre for Advanced Studies, National University of Singapore, 2001).

UNDP *Human Development Report 2000* (UNDP Publications, 2000).

Wang, L.R. *The ROC Report on Women's Rights Indicators in 1998* (Taipei: Human Rights Association of China, 1998).

Watabe-Dawson, M. 'An Overview: Status of Working Women in Japan Under the Equal Opportunity Law of 1985', *Waseda Journal of Asian Studies*, 19 (1997): 41-63.

Westwood, R., Mehrian, T. and Cheung, F. *Gender and Society in Hong Kong: A Statistical Profile* (Hong Kong: Chinese University of Hong Kong, 1995).

Wong, D. 'Foreign Domestic Workers in Singapore', *Asian and Pacific Migration Journal*, 5(1) (1996): 117-138.

Yeatman, A. *The New Contractualism and the Politics of Quality Management, Women, Culture and Universities: A Chilly Climate?* National Conference on the Effects of Organizational Culture on Women in Universities Conference Proceedings, April 19-20, 1995 (Sydney: University of Technology, Sydney).

Yeoh, B., Huang, S. and Gonzalez, J. 'Migrant Domestic Female Workers: Debating the Economic, Social and Political Impacts in Singapore', *International Migration Review*, 33(1) (Spring 1999): 114(2).

Yi, C.C. and Chang, Y.A. 'Change in Family Structures and Material Power in Taiwan', in H.H.N. Chen, Y.L. Liu and M.O. Hsieh (eds), *Families, Human Resources and Social Development* (Taipei: Graduate Institute of Sociology, National Chengchi University, 1995).

Yim, S.H. and Ang, S.L. 'Income Trends: The Gender Income Gap', *Statistics Singapore Newsletter*, 10(3) (1997): 2-6.

Zlotnik, H. 'The South to North Migration of Women', *International Migration Review*, 29(1) (1995): 229-254.

Index